Forever in Love with Jesus
Workbook

Becoming One with the Love of Your Life

Eight Portraits of Christ from John and Hosea

Dee Brestin &
Kathy Troccoli

NELSON REFERENCE & ELECTRONIC
A Division of Thomas Nelson Publishers
Since 1798

FOREVER IN LOVE WITH JESUS WORKBOOK

Published by Nelson Reference & Electronic, a Division of Thomas Nelson, Inc., P.O. Box 141000, Nashville, Tennessee 37214.

Nelson Reference & Electronic books may be purchased in bulk for educational, business, fundraising, or sales promotional use. For information please email SpecialMarkets@ThomasNelson.com.

ISBN 0-8499-4507-0

Printed in the United States of America
04 05 06 07 EB 9 8 7 6 5 4 3 2 1

We dedicate this to STEVE BRESTIN,
a friend of God

CONTENTS

QUESTIONS CONCERNING
THIS CURRICULUM

The workbook you are holding is an in-depth Bible study. It contains ten lessons, each divided into five days. Plan to spend at least thirty minutes each day alone with Jesus. Following are some questions and answers about this study.

Since Forever in Love with Jesus *is the third in a trilogy, do I need to do the first two studies first?*

No. Each study stands alone.

Do I need to read the book Forever in Love with Jesus *before I start the workbook?*

No. The book that accompanies this curriculum is supplementary and therefore helpful, but not essential.

Do I need to watch the DVD?

Please do! All you *must* have for the study are this workbook and a Bible, however, the DVD augments the study enormously. Willie Aames (*Eight Is Enough; Bibleman*) produced the accompanying DVD and did an amazingly creative job. This is not like any Bible study video you have ever seen. We truly had chills because of the presence of God. Though reading the truth is vital, seeing it and hearing it triple the impact. One woman wrote: "After seeing and hearing about the love of God for two days, I couldn't resist opening my heart to Him any longer." The low cost of the DVD will astonish you. Though it is the best yet, with many special features, the cost is low because Willie Aames sacrificed much of his free time for the production. Please, we plead with you: don't miss it! You can purchase the DVD from the Web sites we've listed on page viii or from Christian bookstores.

When do we watch the DVD?

Watch it at the beginning of each session, before you discuss the same session. If you have only an hour and are dividing the sessions for a twenty-week study, watch it every other week. Do two days of the lesson on the week you watch the DVD, and do three days of the lesson and the prayer time on the weeks you do not watch the DVD. The video times vary slightly, but the average time is half an hour. There are questions in the workbook for you to fill out as you listen, but don't discuss them as you watch. Many of these questions are repeated in the lesson, because they are the core truths, worthy of repetition, and you will discuss them then.

Is there any repetition between the workbook and DVD?

Yes. However, because the format is different, it will not be boring but helpful in etching these life-changing truths into your heart and mind forever.

Does the leader need to purchase a separate guide?

No. Leader's helps are in Appendix C of this workbook.

Why do some lessons have Introduction Questions but others do not?

Because the material in some lessons is more difficult to grasp, Introduction Questions are provided to prepare you for comprehending it more quickly. Other lessons need no preparatory questions.

Where can I find the movie for movie night?

Most local video stores have *Tender Mercies* in the drama section. Currently, you can buy the DVD new or used at Amazon.com and BN.com. Also, your library might be able to get it for you through interlibrary loan.

Where can I purchase additional materials from this trilogy?

Your local Christian bookstore or any of the following Web sites:

> www.deebrestin.com
>
> www.troccoli.com
>
> www.thomasnelson.com
>
> www.amazon.com
>
> www.bn.com

Where can I purchase the art appearing in Forever in Love with Jesus?

www.sallybrestin.com (*Aslan I* and *Aslan II*)

www.martinfrench.com (the eight portraits of Christ)

ACKNOWLEDGMENTS

We are so thankful to the following individuals:

MATT BAUGHER:
If you look up *diplomacy* in the dictionary, your name would be there.

SALLY BRESTIN AND MARTIN FRENCH
Beauty and truth are woven so powerfully together in your artistic portrayals of Christ.

STEVE BRESTIN:
Just what the doctor ordered: rich in prayer and rich in courage.

WILLIE AAMES AND HIS TEAM AT OUTPOST
Who better to video a Bible series than Bibleman? What energy and creativity!

JILL WOLFORD JOHNSON
Our Ruth. God can't help but delight in your servant heart.

MARY HOLLINGSWORTH AND HOLLY HALVERSON
Editing needs crediting. It's truly an art and you both are so gifted.

KATHRYN MURRAY
Your gifting at interior design has enhanced the beauty of *Forever in Love.*

DEBBIE WICKWIRE AND DAVID MOBERG
We have been allowed to give our best. You've listened well. You've freed us to fly.

Aslan II
Artist: Sally Brestin (www.sallybrestin.com)

Week 1
TURN YOUR EYES UPON JESUS

_⸺_

Those who look to Him are radiant.

—PSALM 34:5 NIV

MEMORY VERSE:
HOSEA 2:14–15

*S*ome of you have already completed the first two studies in the trilogy of Falling in Love with Jesus. Others of you have just joined us. To all, we say welcome! We are so excited to turn our eyes upon our Lord with you, to help you fall forever in love with Jesus.

For those who have just joined us, it will help you to know that there are three stages in our love relationship with Jesus:

First Love (the euphoric courtship and honeymoon time)

Wilderness Love (the painful time of questioning and doubting your Bridegroom)

Invincible Love (the deep abiding confidence that your Bridegroom will do all things well in His time)

This land of Invincible Love could also be called *Forever in Love with Jesus*

This third stage is the best stage—even better than the euphoric First Love stage—because there is a steady confidence, a sweetness in knowing and being known, and an inextinguishable joy, no matter the circumstances.

The big question is, how can you get to this stage? The key, as we will be explaining, is in the beholding, in turning your eyes upon Jesus.

We are going to be looking at eight very different portraits of Jesus from John and Hosea: portraits as varied as *The Lion, The Bridegroom,* and *The Great I AM.* You will discover that in each of these portraits is both a tender and yet a "terrible" side of Jesus, though the "terrible" side acts always for our good. If you look carefully, for example, at the portrait preceding this lesson, you will see a lion, but hidden in the mane is a lamb who looks as if he has been slain. There will be times when Jesus is a

Lion in your life, tearing apart what is most dear to you, but His purpose is for your good; and His heart—and this you must always remember—is a *Lamb* who loved you enough to be slain for you.

No doubt you wish you could leap from the First Love time with Jesus to Invincible Love, or Forever in Love, but you cannot. Wilderness Love is part of God's refining plan for each of us. At times in your life, Jesus will lead you into the wilderness. While you are there, it's easy to wonder what He is doing. You may try to walk away from Him, feeling forsaken. But those are the very times you need to keep as close to His heart as possible.

That may look different for each of us, but the Bible says, "Draw near to God and He will draw near to you" (James 4:8). You will find that He will come, He will speak tenderly to you, and He will help you to trust His heart. Our key passage for this study, and the one you are to begin to memorize right away, is this one:

> *Therefore, behold, I will allure her,*
> *Will bring her into the wilderness,*
> *And speak comfort to her.*
> *I will give her her vineyards from there,*
> *And the Valley of Achor as a door of hope;*
> *She shall sing there,*
> *As in the days of her youth,*
> *As in the day when she came up from the land of Egypt.* (Hosea 2:14–15)

Think of "the Valley of Achor" as your "valley of ache," as Kathy likes to call it. Weeping endures for a night, but if you lean into God in the wilderness, He will give you joy in the morning. This will not happen, however, if you back away from the Lord; it happens only to those who draw near to Him, who look to Him.

> *Those who look to him are radiant;*
> *their faces are never covered with shame.* (Psalm 34:5 NIV)

The study is divided into five days. We pray that this will become a time you will anticipate eagerly because you are receiving "kisses" from the King. ("A kiss from the King," according to rabbinic tradition, is a living word from Scripture. When a verse leaps out at you and you have the sense that God has spoken personally to you, you have been "kissed by the King.") When you are faithful to spend time with Jesus during the week, you will come to the discussion time glowing with excitement, and it will be contagious. Together, you will help one another fall more deeply in love with Jesus.

If you are a beginner to Bible study, you may find some of the questions challenging. Don't worry! You will get help when you get to the group meeting. We were all beginners once and remember the feelings. What you may not know is how very welcome you are—your newness adds a fresh enthusiasm that recharges those who have known the Lord a long time. You have much to contribute, and we are so glad you were brave enough to come.

If you purchased this workbook before your first meeting with other women, that is excellent. You can do the lesson ahead of time. We suggest that you choose the same place and time to meet with Jesus each day. It will help you develop a habit of spending quality time regularly with Him. If you did not get your workbook before this first meeting, you can get it now and work on it in this session with the other women.

In the appendices, you will find some additional helps:

Appendix A: Worship Choruses
    Prepare your heart by singing Him songs provided here or from your favorite hymn book.

Appendix B: Movie Night
    Plan a movie night midway into the study. This should be a fun time for bonding. Discussion questions are included in this appendix.

Appendix C: Leader's Helps
    This section includes teaching tips and suggestions for answers.

Memory Passages
    This section includes teaching tips and suggestions for answers.

In the back of the book you'll find memory cards. Tear out the perforated memory verse for the week, and place it on the refrigerator or on your mirror. The power to change our lives lies in the very words of God. Keep your heart open to memory work. We've chosen short verses that are easily memorized, especially when kept in front of you. You'll be amazed at how easy it is, and how much it impacts you.

VIDEO NOTES FOR WEEK I

Watch the video first, and then put your chairs in a circle to discuss this lesson. Do not discuss the following video questions. We provide them for those who learn better by taking notes. You will discuss these vital truths in the lesson.

We want you to watch for something funny in video 1. Our key point is that transformation occurs through beholding Jesus. After the video filming, several women said they thought "baholting" must be a Greek word. It's Kathy's New York accent! We laughed and laughed! So, whenever you hear Kathy say "baholt," translate it "behold!"

1.   Dee used to think the secret to being a mature Christian was simply behaving like one, but it is not. It isn't about duty, it's about _____.

2. How can you love Jesus more? By b_____ Him.

3. To behold is "to direct a _____ to an object" or "to _____ the eyes upon."

4. John Piper explains, "Beholding is a way of b_____" and translates 2 Corinthians 3:18 as follows: "We all, with unveiled face, b_____ the glory of the Lord, are being changed into His likeness from one degree of glory to another." Piper continues, "To see God is to be ch_____ _____ _____."

5. We find the same portraits of Jesus in the Old and New Testaments because "Jesus Christ is the same y_____, t_____, and f_____" (Hebrews 13:8).

6. The key passage from this study shows both the _____ and _____ sides of Jesus.

7. "Therefore, behold, I will _____ her, will bring her into the _____, and speak _____ to her. I will give her her vineyards from there, and the Valley of Achor as a door of _____; she shall _____ there, as in the days of her youth" (Hosea 2:14–15).

> To behold Him
> is to love Him.
> To love Him
> is to be transformed by Him.

WARM UP

Share your name and one reason you've come to this group, or one thing that stood out to you from the video. (Or, you can share your name and then say, "Pass." It will then be the next person's turn.)

Though Dee and Kathy are very different, their friendship has become precious to them, and they have experienced the truth of Ecclesiastes 4:9–10: "Two are better than one, because they have a good reward for their labor. For if they fall, one will lift up his companion. But woe to him who is alone when he falls."

How has this been true for you with women you have known through Bible study?

As you look around this group, you may see women quite different from you in age, knowledge, or background. What fears do you have? What joyful anticipations?

Some groups are better than others in helping one another find strength in God. What are some characteristics of stronger groups?

Day 1

We Shall Behold Him

The sweetest times in our lives have come from closeness to Jesus, experiencing a joy that the world cannot ever imagine. Jesus offered us this promise:

> *I came so they can have real and eternal life, more and better life than they ever dreamed of.* (John 10:10 MSG)

(Kathy) I love this version of this verse. So many Christian women yearn not only for what it means to love Jesus and be loved by Him but to experience life to the full, and have "more life and a better life than they ever dreamed of."

Sometimes this kind of abundance can seem beyond our grasp. There are so many frustrations on this earth, not only because of pain and death all around us but because we each have a bent toward sin and a frailty in conquering that bent. Repeatedly, we quench His Spirit. We think, *Will I ever conquer my laziness, my temper, my bad eating habits, my tendency to worry, or my bent toward gossip? Will I ever stop moving into the shadows, thinking I can move away from the Lord who sees everything? Will I ever stop doubting His heart when I go through difficulties?* We have tasted the goodness of the Lord, but will it ever be our true daily bread?

The last couple of years my heart has truly been opened to realize how much more God wants for me—far beyond the point of my salvation. Jesus is the Door, but we can't stop there. Paul wrote:

> *Eye has not seen, nor ear heard,*
> *Nor have entered into the heart of man*
> *The things which God has prepared for those who love Him.* (1 Corinthians 2:9)

You may wonder: *Is that for everyone* but *me? How do I enter into what God has prepared for me? How do I get to this stage?*

There is a simple but profound secret.

Henry van Dyke wrote lyrics to Beethoven's Ninth Symphony, creating one of the most beloved hymns in all of Christendom: "Joyful, Joyful, We Adore Thee." It's as if God gave him a sneak peek into what brings riches to the soul.

> Joyful, joyful, we adore Thee, God of glory, Lord of love;
> Hearts unfold like flowers before Thee, opening to the sun above.

Melt the clouds of sin and sadness, drive the dark of doubt away;
Giver of immortal gladness, fill us with the light of day.

Do you see it? A transformation takes place in those who spend time before Him, adoring Him, *beholding Him*. His light, like the light of the sun, kills the mold and fungus that grows so rapidly in the dark, defeating us, holding us captive. His light truly "melts the clouds of sin and sadness." A simple yet profound truth—one to help you become the woman you long to be.

You may be thinking, *You are telling me that all I have to do is look at Jesus and I'll be transformed?*

Sanctification (the process of becoming holy) is similar to salvation (being forgiven and becoming His child). In salvation, all you had to do, basically, was look to Jesus. Many think, *That's far too simple.* But it is the truth. We are unable to save ourselves. In the same way, we are unable to become holy in our own strength. But as we look at Jesus, learning more about His character, we trust and love Him more. As we do that, we become like Him.

In the video, John Piper explains, "Beholding is a way of becoming," and he translates 2 Corinthians 3:18 as follows: "We all, with unveiled face, beholding the glory of the Lord, are being changed into His likeness from one degree of glory to another."

"To see God" Piper continues, "is to be changed by Him."[1]

Why does beholding Jesus transform us?

Let's consider a practical example. Think about an area where you are prone to stumble: anger, gluttony, gossip—you know what it is. You've tried and tried, yet it trips you up again and again. You know many of the promises that go with choosing the high road. He tells you that He will fill you with joy and peace, that He will set you free. Yet somehow, when faced with a choice, you still often take the low road. How can simply beholding Jesus strengthen you to take the higher road? It's a mystery, but here are a few of the reasons we see that beholding *is* becoming.

First, as you focus on Jesus and get to know Him better, you cannot help but love Him and trust Him more. Slowly, you find that when faced with that temptation, you are more likely to *believe* His promises and do as Moses did.

1. What did Moses do and why, according to Hebrews 11:24–26?

   _____

   _____

   _____

It takes *faith* in Jesus and His Word to pass up sin. The reason we choose sin is because we don't really believe that the high road is the best road. But if you grow in your realization of the wonder and power of Jesus, you are much less likely to be deceived. It's like that game children play of falling backward into someone's arms. Will he catch you? When the catcher is Jesus, you can be sure He will.

Second, and our study in Hosea will impress this on your heart, you will understand how sin breaks His heart. As you love Him more, you will long to keep from hurting Him, just the way a devoted wife doesn't want to hurt a beloved husband.

2. According to the close of Hosea 2:13, what leads to sin?

_____

_____

_____

Third, when you see Jesus as the holy God He is, you are humbled. When you repent, His grace comes flooding in. A biblical example is Isaiah. Transformation occurred when he "saw the Lord seated on a throne, high and exalted, and the train of his robe filled the temple" (Isaiah 6:1 NIV).

3. Read Isaiah 6:4–8 and describe the steps that led to transformation for this prophet.

_____

_____

_____

In the same way, when you see the holy side of God, as Isaiah did, and as you will in *each* of these portraits of Jesus, you will naturally cry, "Woe is me!" The Lord is near to those who are broken over their sin, for He is abounding in mercy. His grace will come to you.

The secret, therefore, as simple as it sounds, is in the beholding, for beholding *is* a way of becoming.

Begin learning your memory passage for this week. If you have just gotten your books, learn the first verse together this week and complete it next week. (Find it in the perforated pages in the back of the book.)

4. Meditate on 2 Corinthians 3:18. Why do you think simply turning your eyes upon Jesus and beholding Him leads to transformation in your heart, mind, and spirit? What reasons can you see?

_____

_____

_____

To truly see Jesus is to love Him. Henry Scougal wrote, "The worth and excellency of a soul is to be measured by the object of its love."[2]

5. When you think about what someone truly loves, how do you think that love impacts her soul and character positively or negatively? Give some examples.

_____

_____

_____

6. As honestly as you can, describe the greatest objects of your affection. (A key is to see what you think about most frequently.)

_____

_____

_____

Day 2

When I Look at You

Imagine that you are going with us and a few of our friends to one of our favorite museums: the Metropolitan Museum of Art in New York City. When we arrive and get our tickets, the woman at the information booth tells us, "We have two exciting exhibits on loan from Israel. If you walk to the left, you will find portraits of Jesus from the gallery of John the apostle, who wrote so much in the New Testament: the Gospel, three letters, and the book of Revelation." Audible exclamations rise from our group, and we *know* we will all be going into this exhibit.

But then the woman says, "And if you walk to the right, you will find portraits of Jesus from the gallery of Hosea—the Old Testament prophet." We are kind of surprised; we look at each other: *What? Christ in Hosea? That book is filled with infidelity, prostitution, oppression.* But we are certainly intrigued.

We decide to split up and meet at the Roof Garden Café for lunch. One group goes to the left, to John's gallery, the other to the right, to Hosea's gallery. Later, over chicken salads and Cokes, we talk enthusiastically about our morning.

> "My favorite in Hosea's gallery was *The Bridegroom*. Did you see His face? It was so full of love . . ."
>
> "Wow! I was just going to comment on *The Bridegroom* in John's gallery. Just seeing Him on that white horse reminded me of Mel Gibson in *Braveheart*."
>
> "Oh—after we finish eating, I want to go there."
>
> "The one I'll never forget from John's gallery was *The Lion of Judah*. The mane was gleaming in the sun, and the eyes seemed to penetrate with an all-knowing look."
>
> "That's amazing. There was a lion stalking by the side of the road in Hosea's gallery! Only he was so frightening."

As our conversation continued, it was obvious to us that the same portraits were in *both* galleries. And then, like a slow and widening light, we realized *why* there was a connection between the two. They painted the same Jesus because "Jesus Christ is the same yesterday, today, and forever" (Hebrews 13:8).

In this study, you are going to be beholding these eight portraits of Christ from the writings of Hosea and John:

The Great I AM

The Word

The Master Artist

The Brokenhearted Bridegroom

The Betrothing Bridegroom

The Redeemer

The Lion

The Way, the Truth, and the Life

Continue memorizing Hosea 2:14–15.

1. Does it surprise you that you can find the same portraits of Jesus in the Old Testament as in the New? Why or why not?

     _____

     _____

     _____

2. Read Luke 24:15–44.
    A. Describe the conversation between the two disciples and Jesus here.

     _____

     _____

    B. What humor do you see in the conversation? How do you think Jesus was feeling?

     _____

     _____

    C. Describe the reaction and emotions of the disciples (vv. 28–35).

     _____

     _____

    D. Can you share a time when somehow you caught a glimpse of who Jesus really was, and your heart burned within you (v. 32)?

     _____

     _____

Finally Jesus appeared to the rest of the disciples. In His resurrected body He could suddenly appear, astonishing them—and yet, it was a real body, one that they could touch and one that could digest fish and honeycomb!

3. Read Luke 24:36–52.
    A. How did Jesus confirm the report of the two on the road to Emmaus to the rest (v. 36)?

     _____

B. In what parts of the Scripture did Jesus show Himself to them (v. 44)?

_____

_____

_____

C. What did He do so they would understand (v. 45)?

_____

_____

4. As you look forward to the portraits of Jesus you will be studying, how do you think beholding Him might impact you?

_____

_____

_____

Day 3

Sometimes It Causes Me to Tremble, Tremble, Tremble

We had no idea, when we began to write *Forever in Love with Jesus,* what lay around the corner for us. We sensed a magnificent staircase spiraling ahead of us, but God gave us only enough light for a step at a time. Now, when we look back, we can identify with the lyrics from that famous old spiritual: "Sometimes it causes me to tremble, tremble, tremble."

Theologians have a term for this: the *mysterium tremendum* or, simply "awful mystery." It is the kind of encounter with God that makes your blood run icy cold. For though God is completely good and loving, He is also holy and just, and when you suddenly realize He is truly present, as close as your very breath, a part of you cannot help but tremble.

(Dee) One of the portraits of Jesus we will study in depth is *The Lion,* who appears in both Hosea and John. As we were writing about *The Lion,* my daughter Sally, who is a professional artist, was commissioned by a couple to paint Aslan, the lion who is a Christ figure in the classic children's series by C. S. Lewis: The Chronicles of Narnia. Sally was inspired by the following conversation that occurs when the children first hear about Aslan:

"Is he a man?" asked Lucy.

"Aslan a man! said Mr. Beaver sternly. "Certainly not. I tell you he is the King of the wood and the son of the great Emperor-Beyond-the-Sea. Don't you know who is the King of Beasts? Aslan is a lion—the lion, the great Lion!"

"Then he isn't safe?" said Lucy.

"Safe?" said Mr. Beaver, ". . . who said anything about safe? . . .'course he isn't safe. But he's good. He's the King, I tell you."[3]

Each morning, before Sally began painting, she prayed that the Spirit of God would take over and flow through her. She wanted to portray both the love of Aslan and the *mysterium tremendum*, the side of Aslan that "is not safe." Like Jesus, Aslan is wonderful in that he is completely good, loving, and merciful. Yet he is also "not safe" in that he is holy, just, and powerful. The White Witch of Narnia and all her evil could not stand against Aslan's power—nor can anyone who persists in rebellion against Jesus. There are also times when, for reasons we cannot fathom now, an omnipotent God may allow Satan or the sin in this world to pour pain and sorrow into our lives.

When Sally completed the painting, she told me she felt the "not safe" side of Aslan had emerged in it, but she wasn't sure she could see the "wonderful side." The morning after she finished, she took it and put it on display at church. A woman came up behind Sally, and placing her hand on Sally's shoulder, said, "I love that tender lamb in your painting."

"What lamb?" Sally thought. Sally has often said that people show her different things that they see in her abstract pieces—unclear images that don't mean anything to her. But when Sally walked over to the painting, the lamb was as clear as the lion. It was unmistakable.

Sally had truly not intended to paint that lamb, but she had prayed continually that the Spirit of God would work through her. When creating the lion's wild mane, she put the enormous canvas on the floor and threw down dark textures for the shadows. Then, as the paint began to dry, she removed some of it with pallet knives, making sweeping arcs to create highlights. In the process, somehow, mysteriously, a distinct lamb emerged. Not only that, he was at the lion's heart, and he looked as if he had been slain. (On the DVD, look for the special feature where Sally explains this with the original *Aslan II*.)

When the Spirit of God gave the apostle John a vision of Jesus Christ and the last days, John recorded what he saw:

> Then one of the elders said to me, "Do not weep! See, the Lion of the tribe of Judah, the Root of David, has triumphed. He is able to open the scroll and its seven seals." Then I saw a Lamb, looking as if it had been slain, standing in the center of the throne. (Revelation 5:5–6 NIV)

When we first saw the lamb, we felt a chill running up and down our spines, for we knew we were in the presence of a holy God.

What we did not know, but, of course, He did is that the very day that Sally delivered her painting to the couple who had commissioned it, she would learn that her dad had extensive colon cancer. The doctors have not given us much hope, but we have hope, because we belong to a God who can and does heal. Though we know we cannot insist, we are crying out for mercy, as He has taught us to do.

As we walk through the deepest valley of our lives right now and realize that the husband and father, this godly precious man, may be taken from us, Jesus feels like the Lion in our lives, tearing apart what we hold most dear. He certainly is not safe. Yet at His heart—and this we must always remember—is the Lamb who has been slain. When I saw the Lamb in Sally's painting, I wept. For whatever awaits us with Steve's cancer, I know that the Lamb of God is at the heart of the Lion of Judah. Jesus is good, He is loving, and if I ever doubt it, I have only to remember that He died for me. The fact that His Spirit led Sally to paint this lamb without her even realizing it is just another evidence of His care, His love, and His mystery.

Review your memory passage, Hosea 2:14–15.

1. According to the following scriptures, what are some ways God may initially draw someone to Himself?
   A. Psalm 19:1–4

   _____

   _____

   B. John 3:8

   _____

   _____

   C. Romans 2:4

   _____

   _____

However, for many of us, it isn't until we see the "other side" of God that we are brought to repentance, the side that makes our blood run "icy cold."

R. C. Sproul talks about "the trauma of holiness," the *mysterium tremendum.* When Isaiah had a vision of the holiness of God, "Every fiber in his body was trembling. . . . Relentless guilt screamed from every pore." Sproul says, "It is one thing to fall victim to the flood or fall prey to cancer; *it is another thing to fall into the hands of the living God.*"[4]

He was frightened—frozen—flattened. What Isaiah *saw* was a *theophany*, or a visible manifestation of God. In such instances it is not unusual for the Lord's coming to be accompanied by earthquakes, smoke, fire, or lightening. As you do this study, ask the Lord to help you put yourself in Isaiah's place, seeing what he saw, remembering that he was just a human being like us.

2. Read Isaiah 6:1–7.
   A. Describe Isaiah's vision of the Lord (v. 1). The Hebrew for "Lord" here is *Adonai,* or "Sovereign."

   _____

   _____

   B. Describe how the angelic beings used their wings (v. 2).

   _____

   _____

   C. Why do you think they had to cover their eyes and feet in the presence of the Lord?

   _____

   _____

When Moses asked to see God, the Lord said, "You cannot see My face; for no man shall see Me, and live" (Exodus 33:20). Likewise, when Moses saw a theophany in the burning bush, the Lord told him to take off his shoes because he was on holy ground (Exodus 3:3–5).

    D. What were the angelic beings crying to one another (Isaiah 6:3)?

_____

_____

Repetition is used for emphasis, as when Jesus said, "Truly, truly, I say to you . . ." But only once in Scripture is a characteristic of God elevated to the *third* degree, and that characteristic is not His love, not His mercy, but His holiness.

    E. What physical phenomenon accompanied the angelic chorus (v. 4)?

_____

_____

    F. What was Isaiah's response and why (v. 5)?

_____

_____

R. C. Sproul explains that the word *undone* is the word "disintegrated." When something is *integrated,* it is put together. It is the same root word that we use for *integrity.* Someone with integrity is whole, or "has it all together." Isaiah was surely such a man of integrity. Yet when he saw the Lord, who is *altogether holy,* Isaiah was "undone," or *disintegrated,* for not even the most noble man or woman can stand in the presence of a holy God.

    G. What did the seraphim do and say to Isaiah (vv. 6–7)? Why was this an appropriate purifying action in light of Isaiah's confession?

_____

_____

3. Many people today complain that church services are boring. Do you think the experience we just read about was boring for Isaiah? What do you think might be missing that would make someone find church or God dull?

_____

_____

_____

God, in His holiness, may be terrifying but never boring. Boredom is caused by a lack of reverence for God in our hearts, in our worship service, or both. How we need to be aware of the *mysterium tremendum*! We can each remember many times when we were aware of this side of God.

(Dee) I was on my knees when I first received Christ into my heart, and I, like Isaiah, had a

glimpse of the holiness of God, and fear overwhelmed me with its icy grip. I saw my depravity and I knew I deserved God's wrath. But then, as in Isaiah's case, grace relieved my fears.

(Kathy) I had just heard the doctor's diagnosis for my dear, young mother: "Six months to a year," he said. I lay weeping on a pew in the hospital chapel, longing for God to come tenderly, to comfort me, to reassure me that He would rescue us. Like a child with a parent, I was thinking, *You've left me all alone. How could you do this to me? How could you let this happen?* In the midst of my despair, He asked me a penetrating question: *Am I not still God?*

How could I ignore the voice of *Almighty God?* I knew Him long enough to know He is the Creator, the Lord of lords, the Holy One. How could I *dare* not answer His question?

How vital to see that the "unsafe" side of God is only and always meant for our good, to cause us to trust Him, to repent, to return and run into His arms. When we do that, He fills our hearts with singing, and we go out glorifying Him.

4.   Can you share a time when you experienced the holiness or the *mysterium tremendum* (awful mystery) of God?

   _____

   _____

   _____

Day 4

Mercy Came Running

Within every portrait there is not only a side that causes our hearts to fear but also a side that relieves our fears—one that fills us with relief, warmth, and strength. We love the way C. S. Lewis described it when the children first meet Aslan, the lion who is a Christ figure:

> Both the children were looking up into the Lion's face as he spoke these words.
> And all at once (they never knew exactly how it happened) the face seemed to
> be a tossing sea of gold in which they were floating, and such a sweetness and
> power rolled about them and over them and entered them that they felt they
> had never really been happy or wise or good, or even alive and awake, before.[5]

What you will learn as you study these eight portraits is that it is vital to see both the terrible and tender sides, for unless we see the whole, we are not seeing the complete truth. In the song "Live for the Lord," Kathy sings, "Our God is love—He also is holy."

When we were seeking God about the scriptural content for *Forever in Love with Jesus*, we both felt drawn to Hosea. It seemed so right, for it is in Hosea where the Lord said, "I will betroth you to Me forever" (Hosea 2:19).

And yet we knew how difficult and how dark much of the book of Hosea is. *How many people would really want to study Hosea? we wondered. After all, along with beautiful metaphors of God's redeeming love are frightening descriptions of His judgment. There are many times when He is the Lion who is not safe. Are women going to be turned off before they understand what we're trying to convey?*

So we withdrew from Hosea. We began to think, *Perhaps we should study the portraits of Jesus that John paints. How encouraging it would be to study the great "I AMs" in John's gospel. Everyone would be blessed by portraits such as I AM the Light of the World, I AM the Good Shepherd . . .*

Yet, *still,* we felt pulled toward Hosea. Which way was God leading?

(Dee) I went to sleep one night saying, *Lord, I want to hear from You. It's so hard to wait . . . Unless You have a better idea, could You show me soon?*

I have found that if I am willing to wait on Him, as hard as that is, He does come. One night I awoke with a thought: *Could it be that the pictures we so love of Jesus from John are also in Hosea?*

I could hardly wait to get out of bed and go downstairs to where my Bible was. I curled up in my green leather chair and opened to Hosea again.

There, in the middle of the night, His Holy Spirit caused me to see portraits that had always been there but now were unveiled. We have talked about "a kiss from the King," when the Word of God jumps out at us, giving us exactly what we need. I certainly was being "kissed" that night. I could identify with the two disciples who were on the road to Emmaus when Jesus opened their eyes and showed them, "*beginning at Moses and all the Prophets,*" pictures of Himself (Luke 24:27, emphasis added). Over and over again, I saw the portraits John painted of *The Redeemer, The Bridegroom, The Lion of Judah, The Resurrection and the Life*—there they were, in Hosea! I could hardly wait to talk to Kathy. *Please, Lord, if this is of You, put this same desire in her. Let her confirm it.*

When I explained to Kathy the parallels between John and Hosea, her eyes widened. She said, "You're right, Dee. Jesus is all over the book of Hosea. I love how tenderly devoted Hosea was to his bride, and yet there were times when he loved her with a very tough love. It is such a parallel to how God loves His church, His bride. And I think women will also understand the personal application—like in Ephesians—'how wide and long and high and deep is the love of Christ.' I definitely think we need to explore that. It will be exciting!"

Today you will see how terrible and tender meet.

1. Review yesterday's passage of Isaiah 6:1–7. How did Isaiah see both the terrible and tender sides of the Lord? How did the Lord relieve His fears?

   _____

   _____

   _____

2. In the famous hymn "Amazing Grace" the lyricist wrote, "It was grace that taught my heart to fear, and grace my fears relieved." If that has been true of you, could you share, in two lines, how it happened and something about the change in your feelings?

   _____

   _____

Meditate on this key passage for *Forever in Love*, and continue to memorize it.

> *Therefore, behold, I will allure her,*
> *Will bring her into the wilderness,*
> *And speak comfort to her.*
> *I will give her her vineyards from there,*
> *And the Valley of Achor as a door of hope;*
> *She shall sing there,*
> *As in the days of her youth,*
> *As in the day when she came up from the land of Egypt.* (Hosea 2:14–15)

3. Has God led you or allowed you to walk into the wilderness at one time or another? And yet, in that wilderness, did He speak tenderly to you and give you hope, joy, and maturity? If so, share something about that time.

_____

_____

_____

Psalm 85:10 has long been interpreted to reflect what Jesus did at the cross for us, both to satisfy God's righteous anger against our sin (the "terrible" side) and to show the mercy that came running on our behalf (the "tender" side). This verse is also what is called a *chiasm* in Hebrew poetry. "Draw an X to link "Mercy" to a synonym in the second line and "truth" to a synonym in the second line as well. The second line reinforces the first.

Mercy and truth have met together;

Righteousness and peace have kissed.

4. What qualities of God in this verse show His terrible side? What qualities show His tender side? What did both sides do on the cross?

_____

_____

_____

5. What would God be like if He were merciful but not holy?

_____

_____

6. What would God be like if He were holy but not merciful?

_____

_____

_____

Some believe that we see the terrible side of God in the Old Testament and the tender side in the New Testament, but that is simply not true. You will see both sides in both, for Jesus is the same yesterday, today, and tomorrow.

As Kathy sings in the video,

> Thou changest not, Thy compassions, they fail not;
> As Thou hast been Thou forever wilt be.

Day 5

He Touched Me

As a preview of what is to come, we'd like to close with an illustration from the writings of Hosea, and then the writings of John. Each of the stories is about a woman who had a sinful past, was confronted with her sin, but then was touched by the Lord. Each is also an illustration of your memory passage from Hosea 2:14–15, which is the theme of _Forever in Love with Jesus._ As you behold Jesus, you will discover there are times when He is tough and times when He is tender, but He is so only and always to transform us into people who are like Him and who go out singing.

We love the metaphors, the word pictures in Hosea. So often our love for the Lord is like "the morning mist," fading even before the sun comes up. But His love for us is like that of Hosea's love for his unfaithful wife: steadfast and eternal.

1. As an overview, read Hosea 1–3.
   A. What, according to Hosea 1:2, did the Lord tell this godly prophet to do, and why?

   _____

   _____

   B. Describe Gomer's sin, realizing it also represents the sin of God's people. Use her own words from Hosea 2:5.

   _____

   _____

   C. What was God going to do to win her back, according to Hosea 2:14–15?

   _____

   _____

Gomer continued to be unfaithful, as we see in Hosea 3. She completely humiliated Hosea by running after other lovers, who had in turn betrayed her and made her a slave. Then they were done with her and were selling her, naked, on the auction block. You would think Hosea would be disgusted with her and walk the other way.

But to her amazement, she saw him walking boldly through the crowd of bidders. She lowered her eyes, ashamed. Then she heard his voice, bidding loudly for her.

Can it be? Why would he take me back?

Then she heard the auctioneer say, *"Sold!"* Though Gomer felt shame, Hosea's eyes were filled with acceptance and love.

He couldn't possibly still want me.

Then she felt his soft cloak being wrapped around her, covering her nakedness.

Jesus loves you so much that He was willing to redeem you. If you have truly been drawn by Christ and have put your trust in Him, He will never leave you or forsake you. Yet there will be times when He leads you into the wilderness. In Hosea, the bridegroom was betrayed, for his bride kept running off with false lovers, so there came a point where he decided:

> *Therefore, I am now going to allure her;*
> *I will lead her into the desert*
> *and speak tenderly to her.* (Hosea 2:14 NIV)

What does the desert look like? It may mean loss and pain. Jesus may allow us to feel the consequences of our sins, or He may knock the props we have been leaning on out from under us—places, positions, or people. We may lose our savings or our health. Yet His purpose is never for evil, but always for good—never to abandon us, but always to draw us near. In the desert, when we are desperate, He *will* speak tenderly to us. And then, one day, He said,

> *There I will give her back her vineyards,*
> *and will make the Valley of Achor a door of hope.*
> *There she will sing as in the days of her youth.* (Hosea 2:15 NIV)

He will turn our "Valley of Achor," or "valley of ache," into a door of hope.

2. Read John 4:1–30 for a similar story from the writings of John.
   A. How was the Samaritan woman's past similar to Gomer's past?

   _____

   _____

   B. How did Jesus make her aware that He knew about her sin, according to John 4:16–19?

   _____

   _____

C. What evidence of faith do you see in the woman, and how did she give evidence of a transformation from "ache" to hope?

_____

_____

Review

Each woman should share, if she chooses, one thing that God impressed on her heart from this study, one way she was "kissed by the King." If He "kissed" you in another way this week (an answer to prayer, an unexpected blessing), record that too. Don't put women on the spot, but give every woman who wishes to share the freedom to do so.

Prayer Time

Each woman should pray silently that the woman on her right will be helped by the Holy Spirit
- to love the Lord
- to love the women in this group
- to understand and apply His Word as she prepares for next week

The discussion leader can close by leading the others in the chorus of "Turn Your Eyes upon Jesus":

> Turn your eyes upon Jesus,
> Look full in His wonderful face,
> And the things of earth will grow strangely dim,
> In the light of His glory and grace.

The Great I AM
Artist: Martin French (www.martinfrench.com)

Week 2
THE GREAT I AM

—⟶ᢙ

He comes as the Door, He comes as the Resurrection, He comes as the Light, He comes as the Way, and the Truth, and the Life, He comes as the Good Shepherd, He comes as the Vine. He is the One who before Abraham was, is.

—R. C. SPROUL

MEMORY VERSE:
JOHN 8:57–59A

*I*t is in the gospel of John that Jesus proclaims Himself, eight times, as the Great I AM. The gospel of John is unique from the other three gospels. That was apparent to both of us, for in each of our lives, the woman who told us about Jesus said, "Read the gospel of John."

(*Kathy*) I was twenty and working a summer office job when I encountered a girl named Cindy. She read her Bible every day at her lunch hour. One day she got out her yellow highlighter and began putting *marks* in her Bible. You've got to understand—I grew up in a home where the Bible was as big as Texas and sat on an end table. You would *dust* it, but you would never *read* it, and you certainly wouldn't *write* in it. As I watched Cindy making huge yellow marks in the Holy Bible, I said under my breath, *Well, she may be religious but she's going straight to hell.*

Yet I knew this girl had something I didn't. She had a confidence and a hope that were foreign to me. By the end of the summer, after I had asked her many questions, she handed me a New Testament and said, "Why don't you read the gospel of John? I'll show you where it is."

(*Dee*) I was a young wife when my sister Sally arrived for the weekend, full of excitement because of her new relationship with Jesus. She asked me, "Who do you think He is?"

"I don't know," I answered. "Maybe a teacher, maybe a prophet. Does it really matter?"

"Oh, it matters," said Sally. "Do you know who the Bible says He is?" Then she followed me around the apartment, reading to me from the gospel of John. When she left, I thought, *Is it true? Is Jesus really God? I don't want to give my life to Him if He is a fairy tale.* Sally had left behind a paraphrase of the New Testament with a bookmark in John.

Kathy and I devoured the gospel of John. We were both surprised and delighted at all He said He was and all He had promised. Through that great apostle, we each came to faith and repentance. What is it about John's gospel that sets it apart from the synoptic gospels of Matthew, Mark, and Luke?

Watch the video first, and then put your chairs in a circle to discuss this lesson. These video questions are here to aid your note taking, but not for discussion.

1. John's gospel is different. It is different from the other three in that "John tells Jesus's story very much from <u>h</u>_____ down" (Darrell L. Bock).

2. John gospel begins with: "In the beginning was the Word, and the Word was with God and the Word <u>w</u>_____ <u>G</u>_____" (1:1).

3. In John we have eight great "I AMs," each one a claim to deity.

    I AM the <u>L</u>_____ of the world. (John 9:5)

    I AM the <u>B</u>_____ of life. (6:48)

    I AM the <u>D</u>_____. (10:9)

    I AM the Good <u>S</u>_____. (10:14)

    I AM the Resurrection and the <u>L</u>_____. (11:25)

    I AM the <u>W</u>_____, the <u>T</u>_____, and the Life. (14:6)

    I AM the <u>V</u>_____. (15:1)

    Before Abraham was, I <u>A</u>__. (8:58)

4. *The Great I AM* began in Exodus: "'I AM WHO _____.' And He said, 'Thus you shall say to the children of Israel, "I _____ has sent me to you"'" (Exodus 3:14).

5. The words for each of the eight "I AMs" are *ego eimi*. These are the same words used in Exodus. Jesus was saying "I AM" twice. Jesus was saying, "I AM God."

    His friends were in _____.

    His enemies wanted to _____ him.

Three Stairsteps

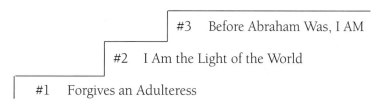

#3   Before Abraham Was, I AM

#2   I Am the Light of the World

#1   Forgives an Adulteress

WARM UP

What has worked for you in developing the discipline of getting your homework done?

Day 1

Heaven Came Down

Dr. Darrell Bock, esteemed expert on the Gospels from Dallas Theological Seminary, says that John's gospel is different from the other three, for "John tells Jesus' story very much from heaven down."[1] Matthew, Mark, and Luke have told us where Jesus was born, how He grew up, what He did while He was on earth—the external facts. But John's gospel is different. There are no greetings, no genealogies, and no gradual explanations leading up to the true identity of Jesus. When the curtain is raised, instead of soft lights and music, we are greeted with a full orchestra, sending tingles up and down our spines: "In the beginning was the Word, and the Word was with God, and the Word was God" (John 1:1 NIV).

God chose John to write "a spiritual gospel," giving us pictures of Jesus as God incarnate. John's gospel, reflects "a Christology of the highest order."[2] Consider the eight great I AMs of John, each one a claim to deity:

I AM the Light of the world.
I AM the Bread of life.
I AM the Door.
I AM the Good Shepherd
I AM the Resurrection and the Life.
I AM the Way, the Truth, and the Life.
I AM the Vine.
Before Abraham was, I AM.

Not only did John make it clear that Jesus was just as much God as God the Father, but also that Jesus is "God with us." He came to be the Light for us, the Bread for us, the Door for us.

1. Look at the beginning of each of the synoptic Gospels (Matthew, Mark, and Luke) and describe briefly how each begins:

Matthew

_____

_____

Mark

_____

_____

Luke

_____

_____

2. How is John's opening dramatically different?

_____

_____

_____

John had a special anointing from God. Darrell Bock quotes Eusebius, a historian who wrote in A.D. 324:

> And the genealogy of our Savior according to the flesh John quite naturally omitted, because it has already been given by Matthew and Luke, and began with the doctrine of his divinity, which had, as it were, been reserved for him, as their superior, by the divine Spirit.[3]

John's prologue, John 1:1–18, which prepares the way for John's gospel, is filled with proclamations of the deity of Christ. If you look carefully, you will also see many foreshadowings of the I AMs. Read the entire prologue.

3. Meditate on John 1:1–5.
   A. How does John 1:1–3 proclaim the deity of Jesus?

   _____

   _____

   B. How is verse 3 a foreshadowing of "Before Abraham was, I AM" (John 8:58)?

   _____

   _____

   C. What does John 1:4 say? As you think through the I AMs, which ones might you see foreshadowed by this verse?

   _____

   _____

D. John's style emphasizes contrasts. What do you see in John 1:5?

_____

_____

Darkness in John's gospel "represents the forces of evil, which seek to overcome it [the Light]. . . . It includes everything that is at enmity with God, whether earthly or demonic."[4]

E. What forces of darkness are you aware of in your life right now that you are thankful cannot overcome the Light of the World?

_____

_____

Day 2

We Are Standing on Holy Ground

Prepare your heart through worship songs (Appendix A). Ask Him to "kiss you with the kisses of his mouth" and have a sense of anticipation.

Spend time learning your memory passage.

The first portrait of *The Great I AM* is not in John, and not even in Hosea, but much earlier: in the book of Exodus. This passage in Exodus you will be studying today is, like John's prologue, considered one of the most theologically important passages in Scripture. What we begin to see here is how tremendously *personal* God is, which is foundational to the portrait of *The Great I AM*. He saw the great need of the Israelites, who were in bondage to the powerful Egyptians, and appeared in the form of a theophany: the burning bush. There He called Moses to be Israel's deliverer, then He identified Himself as the Great I AM. The parallel to John's gospel is that we were in great need, and God appeared or "became flesh" in order to be our Deliverer, revealing Himself, again as the Great I AM. The Great I AM of Exodus is the Great I AM of John. Jesus is the same yesterday, today, and tomorrow.

1. What need does Exodus 2:23–25 identify? How did God respond?

_____

_____

_____

2. In Exodus 3:1–6, describe what Moses was doing, what he saw and heard, and how he felt.

_____

_____

3. Read Exodus 3:7–12.

    A. What did the Lord say in Exodus 3:7–10, and what characteristics of God do you see?

_____

_____

    B. How does this make you feel? What pain does He see in your life right now?

_____

_____

    C. In Exodus 3:11, what question did Moses ask?

_____

_____

    D. In Exodus 3:12, instead of answering Moses's question, what did God tell him? What, therefore, was not the issue? What was the issue?

_____

_____

God is mighty and He is with us. The concept that God will be with us is vital. This phrase, "I will be with you," occurs more than one hundred times in the Old Testament and then is carried through to the New. When Jesus was born, the angels said, "'And they shall call His name Immanuel,' which is translated 'God with us'" (Matthew 1:23). Likewise, the eight great "I AMs" of John are, again, God saying, eight different ways, "I AM with you."

4. Read Exodus 3:13–14.

    A. What question did Moses ask in verse 13? Why was this a logical question, since God had implicitly told Moses that it didn't really matter who Moses was?

_____

_____

    B. Describe the Lord's answer in verse 14.

_____

_____

Please read this next note carefully, for it is vital to understanding the Great I AM.

The Lord cannot be compared to anyone or anything. He can compare Himself only to Himself, so He said, "I AM WHO I AM" (Exodus 3:14). This name is a clear declaration of deity.

What is so fascinating is that this is the same name Jesus used for Himself in John. In each of the eight great "I AMs" in John, Jesus was using the exact same words as in Exodus:[5] *ego eimi.* Both of these words mean "I AM," so, though it sounds strange, Jesus was literally repeating this, saying, "I AM, I AM." They are the same words Moses heard when the Lord said, "I AM WHO I AM." In each of these bold "I AMs," Jesus was claiming deity. This is the prevailing theme of John. W. Hall Harris writes,

John's theology consistently drives toward the conclusion that Jesus, the incarnate Word, is just as much God as God the Father.[6]

Not only is the "I AM" a proclamation of deity, it is a proclamation of the *presence* of God with His people. The verb connotes continuing action—not just past action, but right now, right here. It is as if He is saying, "I AM the *Is-ing One* here right now with you. I AM the same yesterday, today, and tomorrow."[7]

    C. What do the words *ego eimi* mean literally? What do they mean symbolically?

_____

_____

(*Dee*) Tomorrow we are going to look at *The Great I AM* in John's gospel. Kathy and I had one of our typical interchanges when we were talking about *The Great I AM* in John.

"Kath, there are eight of them in John."

"Oh, Dee—there's so many more than eight."

"No, Kath. There are just eight."

"I can think of dozens more."

"What? No, Kath. Don't add to Scripture."

"I'm not adding to Scripture! It's just that when I apply this to myself, He's so much more than eight."

"I don't get it."

And then Kathy looked at me with the childlikeness I have come to love and said: "When my father and then my mother died of cancer, He showed me, *"I AM Father and Mother to you."* In the areas in which I still struggle with chains, He says, *"I AM your Redeemer."* When I battled with depression and bulimia, He said, *"I AM your Deliverer."* As I sometimes struggle with my singleness, He says, *"I AM your Bridegroom."* So many times He has completed the sentence with exactly what I needed and continues to be the Great I AM in everything I need."

What I love about this is that Kathy had grasped the meaning behind *The Great I AM* better than I did—I tend to be more literal. When God said He was the Great I AM in Exodus, He was letting Israel know that He would be with them, He would be their Deliverer. In the same way, as you will see tomorrow, when Jesus said He was the Great I AM in John, He was letting His disciples know that He would be with them—as the Light, the Bread . . . to fill in the gap with whatever they needed. When all seemed lost in Exodus, the Great I AM opened the sea. When all seemed lost in John, the Great I AM opened the grave. The Great I AM is with us, is our Deliverer from what, to man, seems impossible.

5.   What are some ways the Lord has been the Great I AM to you?

_____

_____

_____

Day 3

I Stand in Awe of You

Prepare your heart through worship songs (Appendix A). Be still before Him. This is one of the hardest things to do, but we will be practicing stillness. See if He impresses anything on your heart.

Spend time learning your memory passage.

(Dee) Since my husband's diagnosis of colon cancer, he has had to drop his surgical practice. He has been home, undergoing treatment and spending much time in prayer and in Scripture. I asked him recently what Scriptures have been most meaningful to him. He said, "I have continually been pondering what you told me about *The Great I AM*. It's such a profound declaration not only of the deity of Christ but that He is with me."

This is so meaningful to me as well. I think, *O Lord, You heard the cry of the Israelites and delivered them. Please hear our cry and deliver us.* How comforting to know that we belong to a God of compassion, a God of miracles, a God who will do all things well in His time. Jesus is that God, and Jesus is with us.

We think you will find today's study in John one of the most fascinating you have ever done. With the backdrop of Exodus, and the understanding that each time Jesus proclaimed "I AM" He was also using the holy name of God, study the reactions of either Jesus's enemies or friends. They understood He was claiming to be God. His friends stood in awe. His enemies seethed with anger.

1. Find the eight great "I AMs" of John, and then find a reaction in the context of either an enemy or a friend.
   A. John 6:35

   _____

   _____

   Reaction?

   _____

   _____

   B. John 8:12

   _____

   _____

   Reaction?

   _____

   _____

C. John 10:7

_____

_____

Reaction?

_____

_____

D. John 10:11

_____

_____

Reaction?

_____

_____

E. John 11:25

_____

_____

Reaction?

_____

_____

F. John 14:6

_____

_____

Reaction?

_____

_____

G. John 15:1

_____

_____

Reaction? (Jesus predicted this in John 15:8)

_____

_____

H. John 8:58

_____

_____

Reaction?

_____

_____

2. How can you see, from these reactions, that listeners knew Jesus was claiming to be God?

_____

_____

_____

We are now going to slow down and look at two of the great "I AMs" more carefully in John 8. This chapter begins with an account of a woman caught in adultery. Some of your Bibles may say this incident was not in the earliest manuscripts of the Scriptures. Please know they are not saying this incident is not authentic, but there is a debate about *where* it should occur in the Gospels. There was enough evidence that it occurred at this time that this is where it was placed in the canon.

3. In John 8, Jesus released the woman caught in the act of adultery. This may be a fulfillment of Hosea 4:14. What prophecy did Hosea make there?

_____

_____

_____

4. What does it mean to you that though the world may deal unfairly with women, God will not?

_____

_____

_____

5. Read John 8:1–12.
    A. Whom did the Pharisees bring to Jesus? According to verse 4, in what situation had she been caught? Do you see anything unjust about this?

    _____

    _____

    B. Why did the Pharisees bring her to Jesus? How did He escape their trap?

    _____

    _____

    C. Find everything Jesus said to the woman in verses 10–11. How do you think she felt?

    _____

    _____

D. What "I AM" proclamation did Jesus make? Why is this startling? (See 1 John 1: 5.)

_____

_____

6. Read John 8:13–35.

   A. The reactions to Jesus's statement were strong. Only God is light, and Jesus had used the phrase *ego eimi,* which was also used in Exodus. Jewish law called for two witnesses to substantiate truth. What criticism, therefore, did the Pharisees have of Jesus in verse 13?

   _____

   _____

   B. How did Jesus respond in verses 14–18?

   _____

   _____

Note that Jesus said, "I know where I came from" (v. 14). This is similar to the statement in John 6 when He said, "I am the bread of life . . . I . . . came down from heaven" (vv. 35, 41 NIV). Bock explains that the imagery of Exodus is repeated in the "I AMs" of John. God provided the Israelites with bread, or manna, from heaven. But Jesus is the Bread come down: "I AM the Bread of life." God provided the light, going as a pillar of fire before the Israelites, but Jesus is the Light come down: "I AM the Light of the world."

It is also fascinating to realize that this latter claim of Jesus takes place in the temple, where four candlesticks were lit to remind the people of how God led them with a pillar of fire, of how God, the Light, was present with His people. Jesus claimed to be that Light!

   C. What did Jesus tell the Pharisees in John 8:19? Why is it impossible to embrace God but not Jesus?

   _____

   _____

   D. What promise, and what condition for this promise, did Jesus make in John 8:31–32?

   _____

   _____

   E. How did the Jews respond in John 8:33?

   _____

   _____

   F. Why did they think they had it made? How do you see the same error today in people who were born of Christian parents? Keeping your place in John, turn to Romans 2:28–29 to see how Paul clarified this misunderstanding.

   _____

   _____

G. What evidences did Jesus give them in John 8:34–47 that they did not know God, that they were not truly spiritual children of Abraham?

_____

_____

H. Describe the debate in John 8:48–57.

_____

_____

I. What was unusual about the way Jesus responded in John 8:58?

_____

_____

> This is one of the purest unvarnished declarations of deity that Jesus ever made during His ministry, and it was not missed by His audience, because they took up stones to throw at Him, but Jesus hid Himself and went into the temple and passed through their very midst, and so passed by. They couldn't take His life, but they wanted to take His life at that very moment because they heard in His claim a claim to deity. The Eternal One who comes to this world, He comes as the *Door,* He comes as the *Resurrection,* He comes as the *Light,* He comes as *the Way,* and *the Truth,* and *the Life,* He comes as the *Good Shepherd,* He comes as the *Vine.* He is the One who before Abraham was, is.
>
> —R. C. SPROUL[8]

J. What does their response in John 8:59 tell you?

_____

_____

Day 4
Hosea's Song

Be a responsive bride instead of a dutiful one. Ask Him to "kiss" you today through His Word—and sing to Him!

Spend time learning your memory passage.

(*Kathy*) As I've gotten to know Dee, I have so appreciated her spiritual gifting of proclaiming the truth. She gets so excited about the treasures in God's Word, and God has gifted her to make them clear to others. In her zeal to know the truth, Dee discovers things that many of the rest of us miss. And then she gets so excited.

When we're working together, sometimes she jumps up and starts pacing, going on and on about something that might at first seem dry to me, but then I get it. So often her insights on a passage ignite my passion to know God better, and I find that first-love excitement rekindled in my heart.

Sometimes when she picks me up at the airport in Lincoln (never would I have imagined that I would be making so many trips to the cornfields of Nebraska), she starts right in with some deep theological concept. I'm thinking, *Dee, give me a break here! I've had a long trip. Couldn't we just get a little lunch and talk about something where we don't have to think quite so hard?* But she's so enthusiastic I hate to burst her bubble.

It happened again when she got into the great "I AMs." We were standing at the baggage claim, and she said, "Kathy, the Great I AM is in Hosea too! I was stunned when I saw it—I even called a Hebrew professor at Dallas Theological Seminary when I discovered it and said, 'Is this true? Am I seeing what I think I am seeing in Hosea 2?' And Kath—it's there! Let me show you . . ."

And there, in the middle of the crowd pressing in to grab bags on the carousel, Dee was flipping open her big black Bible and reading to me from Hosea. "Dee, could we just get my bags first?"

(*Dee*) We think you will be absolutely fascinated when you see the Great I AM in Hosea. Today, in preparation, read the opening three chapters of Hosea. It's in there, but it is hard to see. We'll show it to you tomorrow.

1. Read Hosea 1–3 slowly. Write a sentence about the main idea in each chapter.
   A. Hosea 1

   _____
   _____

   B. Hosea 2

   _____
   _____

   C. Hosea 3

   _____
   _____

_____

Day 5
Above All

A good song for today is "Above All."

Your memory passages from weeks 1 and 2 should be smooth.

There came a point in Hosea when God was so angry at His unfaithful bride that He said, in effect, for a time He would *not* be the I AM to His people. Israel had run after other gods because she thought that *those* gods would provide for her. She had not understood that God is above all gods, above all powers, and that she needed to be faithful to Him. Hosea used sexual imagery, characterizing His people as an unfaithful bride.

1. Read Hosea 2:2–5.
   A. The scene was a courtroom. What charges was God bringing against His bride, and what did He want from her (v. 2)?

   _____

   _____

   B. What warning did He give (vv. 3–4)?

   _____

   _____

   C. Why had she run after other lovers (v. 5)?

   _____

   _____

The story that unfolds is that God's bride was persistent in her infidelities. She did not know that God was her *Provider*. Therefore, to bring her to her senses, God was going to *stop* being her *Provider*, stop being like a caring *Husband* to her. It's a frightening passage where, because of Israel's repeated adulteries, God was separating from His bride for a time. Because the reality had gone out of the marriage, He said, "For she is not my wife, and [*I AM*] not her husband" (Hosea 2:2 NIV). Again, the "I AM" is the same phrase as in Exodus, and in John. God would draw her back, and the two would be reconciled, but for a period, He would not be her Great I AM. (We realize this may sound shocking to you, but we will have time to look at it in depth later.)

God intends for His discipline always to restore, not to destroy. He balanced the frightening passages in Hosea with the hope He gave of the day when God's bride would repent and He would say, "You *are* my people," and they will say, "You *are* my God" (Hosea 2:23 NIV, emphasis added). Once again, He would be the Great I AM to them.

This should, however, cause us to sit up and pay attention. If we truly know Jesus, He will never permanently leave us, but He may, for a time, withdraw from us to bring us to repentance. We cannot trifle with God; He is holy, and He calls us to be holy as well. Though here in Hosea He was talking about His corporate Bride, there is an application to each of us. We can't say, "The Lord is just talking to His people in the past; this is not relevant to me personally." He calls each of us to be faithful.

2. In what areas do you long to be more faithful? List them, and then pray, asking the Spirit to give you the desire and wisdom to be true in each of these areas.

   _____

   _____

   _____

How can we be faithful when we have such unfaithful hearts? The same way we do in marriage: the more you love, the less likely you are to hurt your spouse with infidelity. As we behold more portraits of Jesus, we will see how much there is to love.

Review

Each woman should share, if she chooses, one thing that God impressed on her heart from this study, one way she was "kissed by the King." If He "kissed" you in another way this week (an answer to prayer, an unexpected blessing), record that, too, though there may not be time to share that in discussion.

What have you learned this week about the Great I AM that causes you to respect, love, or trust Jesus more?

Prayer Time

Cluster in threes or fours. Each woman, if she is willing, should lift up in prayer an area she wrote about in day 5, question 2. The other women can support her in sentence prayers. For example:

> *Amy:* Lord, I want to be faithful in spending time with You. Show me the best time.
>
> *Beth:* Please protect Amy from distractions and make her time with You sweet.
>
> *Ellen:* I agree, Lord.
>
> *Beth:* Lord, I long to be a more faithful mother, one who blesses her children.
>
> *Ellen:* Give Beth love and wisdom for her boys, and show her what boundaries to set. Give her the strength to keep them.
>
> Silence
>
> *Ellen:* Lord, I long to be more faithful in what I put into my mind. (And so on).

Please Remember

- Do not feel selfish about bringing up personal needs. God tells us to ask for help.

- Keep confidences.

- Don't try to fix the other woman's problem; rather, pray for her.

The Word
Artist: Martin French (www.martinfrench.com)

Week 3
THE WORD

And the Word became flesh and dwelt among us, and we beheld His glory, the glory as of the only begotten of the Father, full of grace and truth.

—JOHN 1:14

MEMORY VERSE:
JOHN 1:1

K athy) So many of us have been brought up with those familiar Christmas songs. I loved to hear that first Christmas song in the mall or on the radio and realize that that time had arrived. I couldn't wait to take the Christmas stuff down from the attic. For many, many years we owned one of those metallic silver Christmas trees—you know, the kind that looks as if its needles are made out of thin pieces of tinfoil. Year after year, we got it out of the box.

Now, most of you know that seeing a wilted real evergreen tree is a sad sight, but picture a wilted tinfoil tree. I still loved it, though. Then I couldn't wait to take out the color wheel. It had four slices of yellow, green, red, and blue plastic that rotated in front of a light bulb and made a faint constant buzzing noise. I still loved it.

I used to say, "Mom! Put on Mitch Miller. We need some Christmas music while we're decorating." I knew every single word and felt a true warmth in my heart—but boy, I sure did not know who I was singing about. The first year that I experienced Christmas as a Christian, I felt like dropping to my knees every time I heard a carol. I was overwhelmed by the good news, the true news. Jesus was real and He was Lord.

This week we will often refer to Christmas carols as we explore the portrait of *The Word.* If you have a hymnal or a book of carols, you may want to begin your daily time with God by singing a few. Consider, as you sing, how often the lyrics express the joy of God coming down to be with us.

VIDEO NOTES FOR WEEK 3

Watch the video first, and then put your chairs in a circle to discuss this lesson. These questions are not for discussion, just to aid in note taking.

Three characteristics are apparent:

1. *The Word* is "God with us" (His supportive presence—as seen in Exodus).

2. *The Word* is a communicator (His holy judgment—as seen in the Torah).

3. *The Word* is *The Master Artist* (His wisdom and creativity—as seen at Creation).

This week, we'll look at all three but study just the first two.

The Word is "God with us."
1. This can be divided into two parts:
    A. The Word is _____.
    B. The Word is God _____ _____.

2. John's emphasis is that Jesus is just as much _____ as God the F_____.

Look at this verse from "O Come, All Ye Faithful," which Kathy sings. See how it combats a common heresy:

> True God of True God, Light from Light Eternal,
> Lo, He shuns not the virgin's womb;
> Son of the Father, begotten, not created.

3. Jesus is <u>be</u>_____ and not created.

4. In Exodus, God fed His people with manna from heaven,

    but in John, Jesus is the _____ _____ _____.

5. In Exodus, God led His people with a pillar of light,

    but in John, Jesus is the _____ _____ _____.

6. In Exodus, God dwelled with His people in the tabernacle, but in John, Jesus is the _____ _____ _____.

    The verb *dwelt* is literally "_____."

The Word is a communicator.
7. When you hear the term *the Word,* some people think the _____ and some people think _____.

They are together.

8. "A great wind blew through the Bible, and lo, it stood up a _____" (E. Stanley Jones).

9. The Word can be t_____ like a sword, but also tender, like the spring r_____.

Those who wish can share one feeling about Christmas carols.

Day 1

In the Beginning Was the Word

(Dee) It's Christmas Eve. I am young enough that Mother is clasping my mittened hand tightly. Enormous snowflakes are falling softly, and I stick my tongue out to catch them. My older sisters are skipping on either side of Dad, who turns, his handsome face filled with joyful expectation, and flashes Mother a smile. I don't know exactly what awaits us, but the excitement is contagious.

Then the steeple appears, and then the stained-glass windows, majestically displaying their grandeur, illumined by hundreds of candles within. I try to peer inside, but all I can see are dim reflections through the glass. "O Come, All Ye Faithful" beckons angelically from organ pipes, floating out between the wooden doors, opened wide. Mother sings along softly:

> Word of the Father, now in flesh appearing!
> O come, let us adore Him.

It is one of my first memories of the majesty of God, of the invisible made visible through the beauty of the night, the music, and the mystery of Christmas Eve. I would be a woman before I understood truly who the Word of the Father, the Christ of Christmas, was.

When my sister presented me with the claims of Christ, one of my first thoughts was, *Do you believe those carols you have been singing all these years?*

The Word is a term only John uses, though the concept is throughout Scripture. The portrait of *The Word* is a rich one, so we will spend two weeks on it. Today we will do an overview of three characteristics of the Word.

The Word is "God with us" (His supportive presence—as seen in Exodus).

Just as with the portrait of *The Great I AM,* so it is with *The Word.* John communicated that not only is Jesus God, but He is with us. *The Word* is John's term for the preincarnate Christ.[1] As in *The*

Great I AM, He is just as much God as God the Father (John 1:1). Therefore, Jesus has always existed, but He left His throne and became flesh in order to be with us (John 1:14). Just as the Lord Jesus was with His people in Exodus, He is with His people today.

The Word is a communicator (His holy judgment—as seen in the Torah).

The Word refers both to Scripture and to Jesus, showing that God's message and God's person are inseparable. He communicated to Moses, to Solomon, to Hosea, (see Hosea 1:1), to John, and to all the writers of Scripture. The Author of the Torah, (the Law, the first five books in the Bible), the Author of the Scriptures, and the One who communicates God to us is Jesus.

The Word is the Master Artist (His wisdom and creativity—as seen in Creation).

Jesus, in the mystery of the Trinity, created the world and all its riches. "All things were made through Him" (John 1:3). Just as He made the world out of chaos, He is making beauty out of the chaos of your life. Just as He brought to completion Creation, so He who began a good work in you will bring it to completion (Philippians 1:6).

Let's slow down and consider these more carefully.

1. *The Word* is "God with us" (His supportive presence—as seen in Exodus).
   A. How does John 1:1 make it clear that Jesus was just as much God as God the Father?
   _____
   _____

   B. *The Word* was John's term for the preincarnate Christ. So when the Lord was with His people in the Old Testament, it was Jesus, in the mystery of the Trinity, who was with them. Find a few examples of how the Lord was with His people in the book of Exodus.
   _____
   _____

   C. What did the Word do that first Christmas, according to John 1:14?
   _____
   _____

   D. How was the Incarnation (God becoming flesh) an example of God being with us?
   _____
   _____

2. *The Word* is a communicator (His holy judgment—as seen in the Torah).
   A. Give a few examples of the Word communicating the holiness and the judgment of God to His people in the Torah. (The Torah refers to the first five books of the Bible, also known as the books of Moses.) Two well-known passages in the Torah are Exodus 20:1–17 and Deuteronomy 6:4–9.

_____

_____

    B. *The Word* refers to both a message and a person. Explain what you think E. Stanley Jones meant when he said, "A great wind blew through the Bible, and lo, it stood up a Man."[2]

_____

_____

    C. How did the Word communicate the holiness and judgment of God to Hosea (see Hosea 1)?

_____

_____

3. The Word is the Master Artist (His wisdom and creativity—as seen in Creation).
    A. How does John 1:3 make it clear that Jesus was present at Creation?

_____

_____

    B. When you think about the six days of Creation, what are some of the things that put you in awe of God's wisdom and creativity?

_____

_____

Day 2

The Word Is "God with Us"

The Word is "God with us." Practice His presence through worship songs, then be still before Him, asking Him for wisdom for your day.

    Spend time learning your memory passage.

The portrait of *The Word* has similarities to the portrait of *The Great I AM*. In both John was stressing that Jesus *is* God, and that Jesus is God *with* us.

    (Dee) This hymn from the ninth century always sends chills up and down my spine (and I'm thrilled to hear Kathy sing it on the video!). We often sing it early in Advent, reminding us of the longing of our ancestors before Christ:

        O come, O come, Emmanuel,
        And ransom captive Israel,
        That mourns in lonely exile here
        Until the Son of God appear.

Emmanuel means, literally, "God with us" (Matthew 1:23). We, as believers, should celebrate the Incarnation, should celebrate Christmas with great joy, for it is the miracle of the Word, of God Himself, coming down to dwell with us. This concept of God being with us is called the *memra,* or the supportive presence of God among His people, as seen in Exodus.[3] God fed the Israelites with manna, yet Jesus was the Bread come down! God led their way with a pillar of fire, yet Jesus was the Light come down! When John said, "And the Word became flesh and dwelt among us" (John 1:14), the verb "dwelt" is literally "tabernacled," or "pitched his tent." In fact, when Jesus took on the form of a man, He Himself became God's tabernacle, dwelling with His people.

This is crucial to understand, because in Exodus, when God came down to be with His people, it is the same concept. He traveled right along with them; He "pitched His tent" with them. *The Message* paraphrases John 1:14 this way:

> *The Word became flesh and blood, and moved into the neighborhood.*

The Word is "God with us." This is the tender side of the portrait of *The Word.* God became a baby in a manger in order to be with us.

Remember to practice memorizing this week's passage.

Read John's prologue: John 1:1–18.

1. List what you learn about the Word.

   _____

   _____

2. What evidence do you find for the Word being Jesus, the Son—and yet as much God as God the Father?

   _____

   _____

3. What irony do you see in John 1:10–11?

   _____

   _____

Here the Greek verb translated "know" means "to recognize someone for who they claim to be."[4]

4. What promise does John 1:12 give and to whom?

   _____

   _____

5. Who creates this spiritual birth? Who does not (John 1:13)?

   _____

   _____

6. What do you learn from John 1:14?

    _____

    _____

7. Find the *memra* or supportive presence of God with His people in Exodus, and then the parallel with Christ in the New Testament.

    A. Exodus 3:20

    _____

    _____

    John 10:25

    _____

    _____

    B. Exodus 12:21–23

    _____

    _____

    1 Corinthians 5:7

    _____

    _____

    C. Exodus 13:21–22

    _____

    _____

    John 8:12

    _____

    _____

    D. Exodus 16:14–16

    _____

    _____

    John 6:35

    _____

    _____

    E. Exodus 25:8

    _____

    _____

    John 2:19–22

    _____

8. Can you give some examples from the past few days of your life of how Jesus has dwelt with you, sustaining you with spiritual bread, light for your path, or strength for the journey?

_____

_____

_____

(*Dee*) When Kathy and I first started writing together, I was always wanting to encourage our readers in the spiritual disciplines of prayer, reading the Bible, memorizing. And Kathy would say: "Dee, let's not do the 'quiet time' thing. I'd rather write about practicing His presence." I've come to see the wisdom in her thinking, for it is so easy for us in our natural depravity to reduce Christianity to a half hour in the Bible in the morning, a few rules (no swearing, no smoking, no sex outside of marriage), and going to church. Instead, the essence of God's heart is not this segmented approach but *Emmanuel*—"God with us." What does that look like? As honestly as we can, let's take a look at moments in a day of two desperate women (Kathy and me).

> 2:00 a.m. (*Dee*): Can't sleep. I wake, as I often do, and immediately begin to worry (about Steve's cancer, about being fat, and about things as trivial as an ugly chair I just bought). I talk to my anxious soul, reminding it of episodes of God's faithfulness in just the last day. Then I pray through Psalm 103. (I memorize because I'm desperate—if I don't pray through Scripture, my mind immediately turns back to Dee, Dee, Dee. But memorized passages help me focus on Jesus and dialogue with Him wherever I am.) I find myself getting sleepy, and drift off remembering Corrie ten Boom's words: "Don't wrestle—just nestle."

> 5:00 a.m. (*Dee*) I am up—I shower. For me, a lot of practicing the presence of God is in not seeing a separation between the physical world and the spiritual world. I enjoy the hot water and soap, the big fluffy terry towel, my soft flannel robe, my steaming mug of coffee, my fragrant pine candle, and my green leather chair. My heart has gratitude for all these gifts from Him. And yes, my green leather chair is where I have my quiet time. (And honestly, I have had many quiet times where I do *not* practice the presence of God. Instead I go immediately to my list of requests and read my chapters and never truly connect with God.) But today, I ask Him to be with me, sing to Him, and truly have a sense of anticipation when I read my Bible that He will "kiss" me. This is an Emmanuel quiet time and it is so good.

> 9:30 a.m. (*Kathy*) I walk out my bedroom door (four and a half hours later than Dee). I turn on all the lamps in my living room. By looking out the window, I know that it's wretchedly cold out there. I'm so glad I'm still in my pajamas. I head for the kitchen for my beloved Maxwell House coffee. Making my coffee in my percolator makes me happy. As I'm going through my morning, I whisper to Him: *Jesus, thank You for this peace. After all I've been through,*

I never take for granted mornings like this when I'm peaceful, I have a feeling of safety in my home, and I look forward to the day. I love You, Lord.

2:00 p.m. *(Kathy)* I was riding alone in my car on I-65 in Nashville. I'd just left a long meeting and decided to check my messages at home. As I was calmly listening through them, I heard the sound of my gynecologist's voice. "Hi, Kathy. Please contact me as soon as you can. I've gotten the results of your pap smear back." Because I lost both my parents to cancer, fear and dread invaded my heart—it was as if I were caught in a net for a couple of minutes and I couldn't get out. But then I remembered to open my mouth and speak. *Jesus, whatever she says when I call her back, I put my life in Your hands. I trust You. Give me the grace for whatever comes my way. And even now, Lord, pour Your blood into every cell of my body.* Oh, the comfort to have Almighty God on my side.

3:00 p.m. *(Dee)* I make a sarcastic remark to our daughter because she mumbled instead of speaking clearly. I see the hurt in her eyes. *Why can't I just speak the truth in love? Why do I have to be mean and snipe at her? She's hurting so much already with Steve's cancer—can't I even give her the grace to mumble?* I gasp for grace the way a dying man gasps for air. I am able to ask sincerely for forgiveness, and she gives it graciously. I seem to make the same mistakes again and again. It seems the only way I can stay in the light is to be continually confessing and repenting. But that's okay—it keeps me in the light where hope and peace are.

Day 3
True God of True God

Sing "O Come, All Ye Faithful," including the verse that is often left out (see it below). Think about the words as you sing them. Ask the Lord to show you more about Jesus.

Spend time learning your memory passage.

Many of us may associate "O Come, All Ye Faithful" with warm Christmas memories, but a Catholic layman, John Wade, actually wrote it in 1743 to combat frequent heresies. It is filled with sound doctrinal truths. The original second verse of "O Come, All Ye Faithful" has been dropped from most hymnals, but it contains the most important truth about the Word:

> True God of True God, Light from Light Eternal,
> Lo, he shuns not the virgin's womb;
> Son of the Father, begotten not created;

O come, let us adore him, O come, let us adore him,
O come, let us adore him, Christ, the Lord.

In this verse, John Wade made it clear that Jesus is true God of true God! He is eternal. He was *not* created like the rest of us; He was begotten. (The idea that Jesus was created was a heresy refuted in the Epistles and in the great creeds. If Jesus were created, it would mean He had a beginning. He did not have a beginning—He has always existed. Instead, the Holy Spirit hovered over Mary so that He became flesh.)

1. Can you explain why it would be heresy to say that Jesus was created?

   _____

   _____

   _____

2. This heresy denies the deity of Christ. It is also heretical to deny the humanity of Christ. He was fully man, therefore He could die for our sins. How does John address this heresy in 1 John 4:1–3?

   _____

   _____

   _____

Another verse from "O Come, All Ye Faithful" that is not always included is this one:

Yea, Lord, we greet thee, born this happy morning,
Jesus, to thee be all glory giv'n;
Word of the Father, now in flesh appearing!

Jesus is Lord, and to Him all glory should be given. The deity of Christ and His atoning work for us are the hardest truths for the modern mind. These are the truths the enemy works day and night to keep hidden from the souls of men.

People are willing to accept Jesus as a teacher, a prophet—but God? They are willing to have Jesus be one way to God, but the *only* way? They welcome Him as a moralist, but as the divine Being who died for them that they might be forgiven? Forgiven? Of what? They might acknowledge frailty in being human, but identifying it as sin is another thing. Why would they need a Savior?

3. According to Hosea 4:6, what destroys people?

   _____

   _____

   _____

John 1:1 has often been turned and twisted, for many cannot accept what it says. Yet, plainly, John begins, "The Word was God."

The biggest and most dangerous trap is the bold lie that Jesus is not God. It is the truth that cults have skewed and the truth the modern mind cannot see. How often do you hear *lies* like these?

"There are many ways to God."

"It doesn't matter what you believe, as long as you believe it sincerely."

"All religions are basically the same."

"It is too narrow to say Jesus is the only way."

"Jesus is a great teacher—but God?"

"Scripture doesn't really claim that Jesus is God."

Many of the cults have specialized in that last one, corrupting the many scriptures that proclaim Christ's deity. And yet it is so clear! Consider just this one verse: John 1:1. Daniel Wallace, in *Greek Grammar Beyond the Basics,* explains that the Greek construction of the phrase "and the Word was God," is the most concise way grammatically to call the Word "God" and yet make some distinction.[5] Jesus, in the mystery of the Trinity, is God.

4. Read Psalm 2.
   A. What was happening in verses 1–3? Whom was being plotted against?

   _____

   _____

   B. How did God the Father respond (vv. 4–9)?

   _____

   _____

   C. What instruction did the psalmist give to the kings of the earth (vv. 10–12)?

   _____

   _____

5. What does Revelation 6:15–17 tell us will happen to those who refuse to acknowledge the Lamb, the Christ, God's Anointed One?

   _____

   _____

   _____

It's interesting to have John talk about "the wrath of the Lamb," for a lamb seems the most tender of creatures. Yet, even in the Lamb we see again both the terrible side of Jesus, the holy and just side, and the wonderful side, the gentle and merciful side.

6. Likewise, the image of a baby in a manger is a tender one, but John gave a dramatically different portrait of *The Word* in Revelation 19:11–16.
   A. Describe the first vision John had when he saw heaven standing open and the name given to the rider. What was He doing?

   _____

   _____

This is a vision of the second coming of Christ. The Word that became flesh as a baby in a manger is now a mighty Warrior against sin, Satan, and Satan's children.

   B. Compare Revelation 19:11 with Acts 17:31. What similar truths do you find?

   _____

   _____

   C. Describe His eyes and what He was wearing. What does His appearance express to you?

   _____

   _____

One day, the One who rested His head on Mary's breast, the One who (as an adult) had no place to lay His head, the One who wore a crown of thorns, will be "trampling out the grapes of wrath and loosing the lightning of His terrible swift sword."

Revelation tells us He will be wearing many crowns, or diadems, woven together into one great crown, representing His complete sovereignty over all. When a king conquered an army, he wore the crown of the king of that army. Jesus one day will rule over all, for He is indeed the King of kings and Lord of lords.

   D. What is His name? How do you think this name is related to the sword that comes out of His mouth?

   _____

   _____

   E. Describe the army who was riding with Him.

   _____

   _____

In *The Vision of His Glory,* Anne Graham Lotz writes: "The army of heaven is the bride of Christ, coming from the wedding feast, still robed in her wedding gown, to share in the glory of her Bridegroom—to rule and reign with Him on earth!"[6]

When we were little girls in public elementary school, we sang the lyrics to "Battle Hymn of the Republic." This song was inspired by the description of the scene John painted of that great and terrible day when Christ returns to do battle with the enemies who have opposed His bride.

We are very aware that the "Battle Hymn" has another meaning, for it was written during America's Civil War and implied that truth was all on the side of the North. We doubt that it was being sung in elementary schools in the South, and the song may still be a source of pain to Southerners. So let us clearly say that it is shortsighted and arrogant to assume God was on the side of the North, for clearly, sin was found on both sides. We recommend the movie *Gods and Generals* to stimulate thought and discussion about the results of this conflict.

Today, in the long aftermath of this war, there are *still* hard feelings, and there are *still* reconciliation efforts going on in our beloved country. We certainly do not want to add to the hurts from this war, and so we prefer to think of the lyrics of this hymn only in regard to Christ's return, when surely, there can be no debate that the truth is completely on His side.

Day 4

The Word Is a Communicator

The Word is a communicator. Be still before Him and see what He impresses on your heart. Ask Him to communicate with you through His Word today. Be expectant.

Spend time learning your memory passage.

When the Word spoke the world into being in Genesis, it was Jesus, in the mystery of the Trinity, speaking the world into existence. When "the word of the Lord came to Hosea," it was Jesus, in the mystery of the Trinity, speaking to Hosea. When the Law was given to Moses, it was Jesus communicating the heart of God to His people. Not only does the Word include the *memre,* or God's supportive presence among His people, but it contains the Law: the words, and the holy judgment of God as seen in the Torah.[7] (The Torah is the first five books of Moses: Genesis through Deuteronomy.)

This communicative aspect of the Word has both a terrible and a tender side. It can feel terrible when it convicts us of sin. It can seem harsh when you read of someone being cast out into the outer darkness where there is weeping and gnashing of teeth. It can be wonderful when we hear how wide and high His love is, when He tells us He will never leave us, and when He promises us that one day, we will no longer weep.

Yet, because God is always good and just, what may seem terrible is not. It is a holy mystery. The picture of Jesus coming on a white horse one day with fire in His eyes and a sword in His mouth causes us to tremble. And yet, that day is when He is waging war against all the enemies of His bride, because He is holy and just. We have come to love this picture of Jesus because we see the sword being used on our behalf and in our defense. The sword, Paul told us in Ephesians 6, represents the Word of God, and we can use it, as well, to defeat our spiritual enemies. When the enemy comes, and he will, we can use the sword of the Spirit, the Word of God, against him.

Review your memory passage.

1. In the book of Hosea, the Word of the Lord communicates and has both terrible and tender sides. Because of His people's infidelities, God brought judgment and discipline into the their lives. How do you see the holiness and judgment of the Lord, as you see in it the Torah, in the following passages?

    A. Hosea 2:2

    _____
    _____

    B. Hosea 2:12–13

    _____
    _____

    C. Hosea 5:14–15

    _____
    _____

    D. Hosea 8:1–3

    _____
    _____

2. Yet even when the Word brings a terrible message to us, it is always for our good. How can you see God's heart in Hosea 11:1–8? What analogy did the Lord make to help you understand His pain?

    _____
    _____
    _____

3. How should we respond to the Lord's discipline and why, according to Hebrews 12:5–6?

    _____
    _____
    _____

4. What instructions from a holy and just God are hard for you, yet you know, in your heart, they are good for you?

    _____
    _____
    _____

5. You can also see the tender side of the Word in Hosea. God showed Hosea that one day His people would respond to Him, would return to Him. What hope do the following passages give?

A. Hosea 2:16-17

_____

_____

B. Hosea 2:19–20

_____

_____

C. Hosea 2:21–23

_____

_____

D. Hosea 14:4–8

_____

_____

In John's final vision he sees the Word returning in all His glory on a white horse. In His mouth was a sword, representing the sword of the Spirit or the Word of God. It is a marvelous picture of the Person and the Scripture combined.

6. In Revelation 18, the harlot Babylon, or the false church, had fallen. Now read Revelation 19:1–10.

A. For what was the heavenly host praising the Lamb (Jesus) in Revelation 19:1–5?

_____

_____

B. What event was about to occur in Revelation 19:6–9?

_____

_____

C. What mistake did John make, and how was he corrected in verse 10?

_____

_____

7. Read Revelation 19:11–16.

A. What do you discover about the second coming of Jesus in Revelation 19:11?

_____

_____

B. Describe Christ's clothing and name as revealed in Revelation 19:13.

_____

_____

C. Who was with Him, how were they clothed, and what were they riding (v. 14)?

_____

_____

The sword in His mouth represents the piercing truth—the Word of God. This sword can be destructive, but its ultimate purpose is to bring order and beauty to the world and to our lives. It is a sword that is used against our enemies, especially the spiritual forces of darkness.

(Dee) As we are battling Steve's cancer, I have found that this is indeed a spiritual battle. It is as if the enemy is pushing in every window, throwing seeds of doubt, despair, and discord. I am most vulnerable to his cruel and hateful attacks in the night. As I lie awake in the dark, he begins to taunt, _How will you possibly get along without Steve?_ My tears start, and soon I have to leave Steve's dear sleep-warm body and go to another room, so that my sobs will not awaken him.

One night, I e-mailed my friend Jan Silvious and said, "I am praying with my whole heart for healing, but I realize God is not obligated to heal Steve. When I think about that, I begin to sob. And then I think, _Well—but what if God has mercy and heals Steve? Then all these tears, all these sleepless nights, and all these days when I am walking about like a limp rag are in vain._" Jan e-mailed back with a verse that has sharpened my sword, and I am now pulling it out of my covers when the enemy comes in the night.

> _Give your entire attention to what God is doing right now, and don't get worked up_
> _about what may or may not happen tomorrow. God will help you deal with whatever_
> _hard things come up when the time comes._ (Matthew 6:34 MSG)

Amazingly the enemy flees out into the black night where he belongs with the bats. My tears stop. And I have the energy to be the kind of wife Steve so needs me to be. In this valley, I am memorizing like crazy so that I am ready for the enemy's attacks wherever I am: doing housework, in the shower, biking, or in bed. I am wielding my sword, and the enemy is fleeing. The Word is a weapon against the enemy and a comfort to me in my time of need.

8. Share a time when the Word of God has brought you comfort or supplied you with help against temptation or the enemy.

_____

_____

_____

He Will Come to Us Like the Spring Rains

Prepare your heart through worship songs, thinking about the words.

Spend time learning your memory passage.

Next week we will look at how the Word is the Master Artist. Today we will continue to explore the Word as a communicator, and the effect this can have in our lives. Hosea compared the power of the Word to the spring rains and how they bring forth fruit from the earth.

(Dee) My business manager, Jill, is married to Keith Johnson, a farmer. Recently when she arrived at my home she looked out and saw that it had begun to rain. She let out a little cry of joy, saying, "Praise God," and walked out on the back porch. I knew what she was feeling, reveling in the steady downpour. She knows how hard her husband works every day, from dawn to dusk, and she has also seen all that work wiped out by a devastating drought.

In other words, Jesus, as the Word, is here with us and is filled with wisdom, power, and comfort. And as He, through His Spirit and His Word, falls upon hearts eager to receive, He cannot help but produce fruit.[8] Hosea talked about the Lord coming to us "like the spring rain."

1. What metaphor does Hosea 6:3 use for the knowledge of God? What do you learn from this?

   _____

   _____

   _____

2. Isaiah 55:10–11 extends this metaphor. To what did Isaiah compare the word that goes forth from God's mouth? What truths do you learn from this?

   _____

   _____

   _____

Do you see? Once rain and snow have started falling, they never suddenly reverse their course. In the same way, once the Word has started speaking into our hearts, He doesn't all of a sudden, like a child, say, "I take it back." Once He has started a new creative work in us, He will bring it to completion.

3. Psalms 1 and 2 are considered to be the introduction to all of Psalms. What similar truths do you see in Psalm 1 to the metaphor we have been considering?

   _____

   _____

   _____

4. Review your memory passages from these three weeks. If they are shaky, take time now to learn them well. Write them down, then meditate on them, allowing the water of the Word to sink deep. What thoughts do you have about each as you meditate?

_____

_____

_____

5. Can you share a time when the Word profoundly spoke to you, watering you, and bearing fruit in your life?

_____

_____

_____

It should truly give us hope that God, the Word, who created this amazingly beautiful world out of chaos is the same Word who can take the chaos of our lives and create persons of spiritual beauty.

Review

1. What have you learned this week about the Word that you think you will remember? Were you "kissed" by the King?

Prayer Time

One of the most powerful ways to pray is to pray through Scripture. Cluster in threes or fours. Open to Psalm 119, the psalm that exalts God's Word, and choose an octrain (a segment of eight verses). Take turns with passages, praying through them. For example, consider the first half of the fifth octrain:

Mary

The verse: "Teach me, O Lord, to follow your decrees; then I will keep them to the end" (v. 33 NIV).
The prayer: "Lord, teach me to obey Your Word, help me keep Your commandments all my life."

Ellen

The verse: "Give me understanding, and I will keep your law and obey it with all my heart" (v. 34 NIV).
The prayer: "Please open my eyes, and help me understand what I read and to fully obey."

Amy

The verse: "Direct me in the path of your commands, for there I find delight" (v. 35 NIV).

The prayer: "Yes, Lord, bring to my remembrance Your commands, and guide me, and give me the delight of obedience."

Mary

The verse: "Turn my heart toward your statutes and not toward selfish gain" (v. 36 NIV).

The prayer: "Please put the desire for Your Word in my heart, and take away the desire for selfish things."

The Master Artist
Artist: Martin French (www.martinfrench.com)

Week 4
THE MASTER ARTIST

Oh Lord, how manifold are Your works! In wisdom You have made them all. The earth is full of Your possessions—This great and wide sea, In which are innumerable teeming things.

—Psalm 104:24–25

MEMORY VERSE:
JOHN 1:2–3

Dee) When my sister came to visit and followed me around with her big black Bible, it was a huge surprise to me when she said Jesus made the world. "Jesus wasn't alive then," I said, naively.

"Yes, He was," my sister said, "It says that the Word was with God in the beginning. He has always existed. Look," she said, thrusting her massive Bible under my nose. She pointed at a verse:

> *All things were made through Him,*
> *and without Him nothing was made that was made.* (John 1:3)

That was a lot to ponder. It still is.

This week we are continuing with the portrait of *The Word* with a portrait within a portrait. Within the portrait of *The Word* is *The Master Artist.* To review:

1. *The Word* is "God with us" (His supportive presence—as seen in Exodus).

2. *The Word* is a communicator (His holy judgment—as seen in the Torah).

3. *The Word* is the Master Artist (His wisdom and creativity—as seen at Creation).

There are so many aspects to the portrait of *The Master Artist* within *The Word.* An intriguing one is that since since we are made in His image, each of us, like Him, has a creative bent. Some women love to create flower beds of brilliant colors. Some women love to create a dinner that tantalizes all the senses. Some women love to create a "look" and enjoy all the shopping that goes along with it. Some women are the kind of fun moms who end up having all the neighborhood kids at their house because they dye Easter eggs with them or help them turn the basement into an Indian reservation, complete with cardtable teepees and broomstick horses.

(Kathy) I love to create an atmosphere in my home and be surrounded by beauty. I remember when this yearning was awakened. I was in second grade, and we were going on a field trip. I would have loved to be going to the New York planetarium or the Museum of Natural History. Those were exciting not only because of what we'd see but because they were in New York City. But here we were, piling on a bus, going to a home of a president. I had in my heart that it was probably going to be pretty boring, but at least I wasn't going to be stuck in a classroom.

My mother was along as a teacher's helper because my mother was *always* along.

We drove onto an estate that was lined by majestic trees and landscaped gardens. There stood a twenty-three-room Victorian structure overlooking Oyster Bay Harbor and Long Island Sound. It was called Sagamore Hill, home of President Theodore Roosevelt. It served as his summer White House. There I was, a wide-eyed little girl walking into this house that had velvet ropes across the doorway of every room. It didn't take me too long to realize that though I couldn't step into the room, I could step into the memory of it.

Something immediately happened in me. I was totally taken by the surroundings: the high ceilings, the intricate craftmanship in the heavy furniture, the solid silver candelabras, the white porcelain tubs with claw feet, the wood floors that creaked (even the sound warmed my soul), and the smell of "old." (There was an abundance of wood—mahogany, black walnut—all kinds of worn leather and velvet. There were books, quilts, and paintings. How could there not be an aroma of life?)

I kept thinking, *These windows have seen so much. These floors have felt so much. The walls have heard so much.* Little did I know at that moment, I fell in love with antiques and all the charm of that era. It all survived and had a story to tell.

We piled into the bus at the end of the day, and everyone immediately started chatting. (You can picture a bus full of second-graders: even after a long day, though tired, they're still rambunctious.) In contrast, I sat quietly next to my mother and stared out the window with such a sorrow in my heart. Leaving Sagamore Hill was like leaving a friend. I couldn't have articulated it at seven, but the beauty, and romance, and simple joy of old-time America became ignited in my heart.

My mood was pretty obvious, so my mom asked me what was wrong. All I could do was cry. I'm sure she thought something was desperately wrong, but little did we know, because I was far too young to express it, that a yearning for truly experiencing the passions of life was being awakened. I laid my head on her lap and sobbed.

Poor Mom. How do you console a child who is crying, not out of hurt but out of that deep part that has been designed to feel, and be aware, and breathe in all the riches of God's creation? When God knit me together in my mother's womb, He made me an artist. This has nothing to do with me, but it has everything to do with my Creator and how He blessed me. He gave me, even as a little girl, eyes to see and a longing to create beauty.

(Dee) To walk into Kathy's new home in Nashville is almost a holy experience. God has given her such an eye for how to create ambiance. She's constantly humbled at the way He has provided for her in her singleness. I was at the housewarming her best friends threw for her, and as they thanked God for this provision, Kathy wept. It has become a place of refuge for her in the midst of her hectic traveling schedule. Kathy planned it all: the colors, the rich woods, the artwork, the leather chairs. Truly, it is a sanctuary, and Kathy has affectionately named it "Gracie."

Another aspect to the Word as a Master Artist is that He is a painter and a potter, two concepts this lesson will explore.

You may not have a gift for interior decorating or storytelling or cooking, but you have a creative bent somewhere. Again, each of us is made in the image of the Master Artist, and it is good to think about how we are like Him in the creative aspect. We'll consider this tomorrow, and then, as the week progresses, look at some other aspects about the Master Artist that impact each of us profoundly.

VIDEO NOTES FOR WEEK 4

Watch the video first, and then put your chairs in a circle to discuss this lesson. These questions are for taking notes, not for discussion.

1. Christ is a painter of _____.

2. Jesus spoke in _____ and the prophets used _____
   _____.

   Jeremiah wore a _____.

   Isaiah ate a _____.

   Ezekiel saw a graveyard of _____ come alive.

3. Hosea's life was a full-length mural of an _____ bride and a
   _____ husband.

4. Christ is a potter of clay. A potter continually sprinkles _____ on the clay
   to keep it pliable.

WARM UP

In what areas of your life do you express your creative bent?

Day 1

For the Beauty of the Earth

(Dee) One of my favorite hymns is "For the Beauty of the Earth." In fact, my precious daughter-in-law Julie, who has so many creative gifts, painted an old coffee table for me with women dancing in a meadow filled with flowers. All around the sides, in calligraphy, she painted the lyrics of this lovely hymn:

For the beauty of the earth,
For the glory of the skies,
For the love which from our birth
Over and around us lies.

Consider the lyrics to this old hymn. Creation is evidence of His love all around us. And how amazing it is that the Word who created the lilies of the field, the teeming fish of the sea, and the stars of the night is also at work refashioning us!

How encouraging that the Master Artist who used words to command beauty out of chaos in the first Creation, also uses His Word to bring beauty out of chaos in us. Another important truth to ponder is that the Artist who created the stars, the sunflowers, and the sea out of nothing is at work in your life. No matter how you've blown it, no matter how little you feel you have to offer, He has the power to transform you.

A man who explains this so well is Charles Spurgeon. Spurgeon is called "the preacher of preachers" and lived in England in the 1800s. Twice a week he preached in a sanctuary that held eight thousand (without a mike!), and people lined up for blocks in hopes of getting a seat. If we had lived then and there, we definitely would have been in that line! The eloquence, the romance, and the power behind his words existed only because God was with him. Read carefully this excerpt from a sermon delivered on a Thursday evening, January 23, 1873:

> We cannot tell how the Spirit of God brooded over that vast watery mass. It is a mystery, but it is also a fact. . . . These real facts may illustrate the work of God in the new creation. . . . The work of the Holy Spirit in the soul of man is comparable to his work in creation. . . . That same Master-Artist has drawn lines and curves of spiritual beauty upon the souls of the redeemed. . . . The very first act in the great work of the new creation is that the Spirit of God moves upon the soul as he moved upon the face of the waters . . . and where the Spirit came, the work was carried on to completion.[1]

1. We usually think of God the Father creating the world. But all three Persons of the Godhead were there. What evidence in the following verses can you find for Jesus's being present?
   A. John 1:1–3

   _____

   _____

   B. Colossians 1:16

   _____

   _____

2. As you think about Jesus being with God the Father and God the Spirit at Creation, saying, "Let there be light," and speaking the world into being, what is one reason you can see for John calling Jesus "the Word?"

_____

_____

_____

3. In Hebrews 1:10, God the Father is speaking to God the Son. What do you learn from this verse?

_____

_____

_____

4. What does Philippians 1:6 say?

_____

_____

_____

5. What does it mean to you that the One who created the world is at work in you, bringing you to completion?

_____

_____

_____

6. So often we pray for everything except our own character. In your personal time with God, pray through the following verses, asking Him to re-create you.
   A. Psalm 119:73

   _____

   _____

   B. Romans 8:28–29

   _____

   _____

   C. Isaiah 45:9–12

   _____

   _____

God is at work in you, molding you, shaping you into a vessel of beauty.

We love the movies such as _Cinderella, Sabrina,_ and _My Fair Lady,_ where a woman is transformed through the help of an "artist." We have a much more competent Artist at work on us who can do amazing things if only we can learn to yield to Him. In the story of Hosea, He was doing the makeover of makeovers. Gomer was unfaithful, rebellious, and deceived. Gomer's story is our story, for Gomer not only represents God's people, but everyman.

Beginning tomorrow, we will look deeply into this Cinderella story.

Day 2

The Word Is a Painter of Pictures

Prepare your heart with worship and meditation on your memory work.

To review, within the portrait of *The Word* is *the Master Artist*. It is also true that within the portrait of *The Master Artist* are two more portraits: *Painter* and *Potter*.

THE MASTER ARTIST

A Painter of Pictures

God will paint pictures and parables to turn the light on inside our minds and communicate His heart to us. In Hosea He painted a picture that penetrates in a way mere words could not. He commanded Hosea to live out a parable before the eyes of His people so that they could understand that they, like Hosea's wife, are unfaithful brides, and that God, like Hosea, is a brokenhearted lover.

Potter of Clay

He will be intensely involved, skillful, and sovereign over our lives, as is a potter with his clay. He will use the water of the Word, as the potter uses water with the clay, to keep us pliable and to conform us to the image of Christ. He will take an immoral woman, like Hosea's wife, and fashion her into a vessel of honor. He is doing the same with us.

They say a picture is worth a thousand words, and we are so thankful that God led us to exactly the right artist for the eight portraits we have of Jesus in this curriculum. Martin French has captured so much emotion in each of his drawings. Though we can say, "Jesus is the Potter," how much more powerful to actually *see* the firm muscle tension in His hands, the concentration in His eyes, the love in the whole process. It makes us more willing to yield!

(*Kathy*) Just as actual pictures turn the light on, word pictures can bring illumination. I know that some of the most powerful songs the Lord has given me are filled with word pictures. One lyric painted such a word picture that lives were saved and hearts tormented by shame and guilt were finally set free. It's called "A Baby's Prayer." I feel as if the divine hand of God truly penned this one.

A BABY'S PRAYER

I can hear her talking with a friend,
I think it's all about me.
Oh how she can't have a baby now,
My mommy doesn't see
That I feel her breathe,

I know her voice,
Her blood—it flows through my heart.
God, You know my greatest wish is that
We'd never be apart.

But if I should die before I wake,
I pray her soul you'll keep.
Forgive her, Lord,
She doesn't know
That You gave life to me.

Not only have I held babies in my arms that were scheduled to be aborted, but I have seen the light come back on in women's eyes when they've allowed God to release them from that choice. One extra blessing has come that I didn't even plan on: the song's touching the thousands of women who have had miscarriages. The last verse says this:

On the days when she may think of me
Please comfort her with the truth
That the angels hold me safe and sound,
'Cause I'm in heaven with You.

(Dee) In *The Five Love Languages,* Gary Smalley and John Trent recommend using word pictures to help others understand your feelings. When we were flying home from Thailand with our newly adopted twelve-year-old daughter, Steve started talking about how cute the little boys were in the orphanage. With five children and a ministry, I was feeling overwhelmed. Was he really thinking I could handle more? How could I help my left-brained husband understand? I used a word picture!

"Honey, see that little handle out on the wing? Imagine I am out there, hanging on for dear life, but I am flapping around in the wind and I may lose my grip. I want to keep up with you, but I think I'm going to slip and plummet to my death."

"Is that how you are feeling?"

"Bingo."

A word picture helped Steve understand my heart. I have learned, from the Lord's model, that if I really want to persuade someone of something, if I really need him to understand, I must come up with an effective word picture.

Word pictures have power. Let's consider some the Lord paints.

1. Consider the particular "I AM" in John 10:11–18. Jesus could have simply said, "I will take care of you." Instead He painted a memorable word picture. What is it and why is it more meaningful than a simple statement?

   _____

   _____

   _____

2. When David committed adultery, God sent Nathan with a word picture (2 Samuel 12:1–15). Why do you think God did this instead of having Nathan confront David directly with His sin?

_____

_____

_____

3. The prophets often used object lessons to portray God's truth, just as the Gospels use parables. Jeremiah, "the weeping prophet," wore a yoke around his neck, Ezekiel actually ate the word of God. Describe two other particular pictures the Lord painted through Ezekiel, and explain why a picture was more powerful than a simple statement.
   A. Ezekiel 12:1–7

_____

_____

   B. Ezekiel 37:1–14

_____

_____

One of the most powerful word pictures in Scripture is the full-length mural that the Lord had Hosea paint with his lifelong marriage to an adulterous woman. One commentator writes:

> God could have simply declared: Israel is like a wife to me, an adulterous wife. Instead, He used Hosea to act out the treachery in real life and to show in living color, God's fury, His jealousy, and above all else, His love for His people.[2]

There are those who say, "But God would not command a prophet to marry an immoral woman because He wouldn't link a believer with an unbeliever." We understand the dilemma. It is true that He tells us not to marry unbelievers (see 2 Corinthians 6). However, there are "godly prerogatives." God is allowed to have some feelings and actions that we are not. For example, we are not to be jealous, but God, because He is without sin, can and is jealous for our devotion. We are not to take vengeance on one another, but God can and will, because He is holy. Those are "godly prerogatives." These are negatives to us, but with perfect holiness God can use them wisely and justly.

He can, because He is God, ask a prophet to marry an immoral woman in order to paint a picture, but that certainly does not give us a license to marry unbelievers. James Montgomery Boice wrote:

> If Hosea's story cannot be real (because "God could not ask a man to marry an unfaithful woman"), then neither is the story of salvation real, because that is precisely what Christ has done for us. He has purchased us for himself to be a bride "without stain or wrinkle or any other blemish, but holy and blameless" (Eph. 5:27), and he has done this even though he knew in advance that we would often prove faithless.[3]

4. Write down how you would answer someone who says, "Hosea married an unbeliever, so I can too."

_____

_____

_____

5. Summarize some of the reasons that the Word is a painter of pictures.

_____

_____

_____

6. Think about something that is very important to you that you have been unable to communicate clearly to someone. Can you think of a vivid word picture that might help him or her understand the emotion behind your words? If so, share it briefly.

_____

_____

_____

Day 3

The Full-Length Mural of Hosea

Turn to Appendix A and sing to the Lord.

Can you imagine how shocked the Israelites were when they saw Hosea and Gomer together? Imagine that you are at a dinner table with several people, and there is a pastor across from you who reminds you of a young Billy Graham. He's substantial and well spoken. He's extremely wise and sensitive to the people around him.

Next to him is a woman who is obviously unsophisticated, chewing gum as she talks loudly. Her makeup is caked on in layers, and her cheap perfume dominates the table. She is wearing a very low-cut dress and she leans over to talk to everyone, flirting with the men. *Who is she?* Your jaw drops as the pastor puts his hand over hers and says, "I'd like to introduce you to my *wife . . .*"

Perhaps this is how the Israelites reacted when Hosea introduced Gomer. *Why would a godly prophet like Hosea marry such a blatantly promiscuous woman?*

No doubt, God's command also came as a surprise to Hosea himself. Preacher E. F. Bailey imagined the interaction between the Lord and Hosea the day "the word of the Lord" came to the unsuspecting prophet, telling him to marry an adulterous woman:

I was making my way back home from one of my many crusades when I descended the heights of Mount Tabor. Suddenly I was apprehended by a strange and invisible presence. . . . I was at once both terrified and fascinated. . . . His voice came to me. . . .

"Hosea, I must speak to you concerning the infidelity of my people.

"You remember our contractual agreement: that Israel would be my people and and that I would be her God. But now, Hosea, because of her apostasy, idolatry, and immorality, her goodness is as the morning dew . . . She has fractured our friendship, she has ruptured our relationship."

His voice was the voice of one who had experienced excruciating pain—pain only known to those who have had their love rejected. . . .

"Hosea, I want you to get married. I want you to be my living allegory. . . .

"Hosea, I tuned in to several of your last crusades and as I listened to you it was obvious to me that you're not quite ready. . . . You were knowledgeable in theology, eloquent in speech . . . but there was something missing, . . . Hosea, in order to get you ready I am going to send you through the crucible of domestic difficulty."

"Married?" I said. That's not so bad. Especially when you have an omnicompetent, personal God selecting the bride. . . . " I said, "God, it's interesting that you would bring that subject up. Just the other day I was having a conversation with myself and I said, 'Prophet, it's time for you to take on a wife . . .' There is this young lady I've been watching—and I know You know who she is. She comes from an orthodox Jewish background, she's a prophet's child, she comes to all of my crusades. . . . Oh, she'll make a great prophet's wife. . . ."

"Hosea, she's not the one I have in mind. The girl that I have in mind for you is not out of a prophet's family. She's not orthodox. In fact, Hosea, the girl I want you to marry is a pagan prostitute." [4]

There is humor in E. F. Bailey's presentation—unless, perhaps, you have been the victim of infidelity. Then it becomes deadly serious.

This was a *life* sentence, for Hosea prophesied for seventy years, and all during that time, the wife he loved was breaking and rebreaking his heart. One commentator writes,

> Hosea is one of the most emotional books in the Bible, an outpouring of suffering love from God's heart. This shows in the writing, which jumps impulsively from one thought to the next. Read a chapter dramatically aloud, and you will get this sense. It is almost like listening in on a husband-and-wife fight. [5]

When you read Hosea's story, you can almost see the tear stains on the pages. The Lord was trying to penetrate His people's dull hearts, to help them wake up and see how their unfaithfulness had caused Him grief.

1. Put yourself in Hosea's place. How do you think you would have felt about the Lord's plan for your life?

_____

_____

_____

In Hosea 1:1, the word of the Lord came to him, and in verse 2, literally, the Lord "began to speak by Hosea." This is the unique miracle that happened to and through the prophets, whose books make up over a quarter of the Old Testament.

Read Deuteronomy 18:17–22.

2. Why, according to Deuteronomy 18:18, are prophets able to boldly say, "Thus says the Lord"?

_____

_____

_____

3. False prophets abounded in Israel. According to Deuteronomy 18:21–22, how could the Israelites know if a prophet was truly speaking the word of God?

_____

_____

_____

Each prophet had to give a *near* prophecy so his credentials could be checked. For example, the prophecy of Hosea 1:7, that Judah would be rescued *not* by military might but by God, was fulfilled (2 Kings 19:32–36). This miracle established Hosea's credentials.

4. In 1 Peter 1:10–12, why did the apostle tell us to pay attention to these Old Testament prophets?

_____

_____

_____

5. How did Hosea respond to the word of the Lord (Hosea 1:3)? What does this tell you about him?

_____

_____

_____

6. Now put yourself in the place of the Israelites. What feelings might they have had upon seeing the following scenes?

A. When they first saw Hosea and Gomer as husband and wife:

_____

_____

B. When they realized that immoral Gomer represented them and their unfaithfulness:

_____

_____

C. When they saw Hosea's heart being broken and broken again:

_____

_____

D. When they saw the pain of Gomer's life—how her lovers put her up, naked, to be sold at the slave market:

_____

_____

E. When they saw Hosea's persistent faithfulness to his unfaithful wife—how he bought her back and covered her:

_____

_____

7. How does love keep a person faithful to another, even in the face of temptation?

_____

_____

_____

8. What does this tell you about how leading a victorious life?

_____

_____

_____

9. Think about each of the word pictures in question 6. Is the Lord speaking through them, in any way, to you personally? If so, how?

_____

_____

_____

10. How will you respond?

_____

_____

_____

Scattered! Not Pitied! Not My People!

Today's passage could be disturbing, but it is not the end of the story. Meditate on 1 Peter 2:9–11 and thank God for the truths in it. Sing some worship songs about God's love.

We are a stiff-necked and stubborn people, but the Word paints pictures to penetrate those hard hearts. This is what He was doing in Hosea.

Hosea's mural continues to unfold with the births of three children. Read Hosea 1:1–9. The first child's name is the most difficult, but fascinating: Jezreel.

1. What prophecy does Hosea make in Hosea 1:4?

    _____

    _____

    _____

When Jehu was king of Israel, he was ordered to avenge the deaths of the prophets. However, in his zeal, he exceeded Elijah's instructions from God.[6] There was terrible bloodshed in the valley of Jezreel, and in Hosea, God's anger against this act was revealed.

In our natural depravity, because of our lust for power and our lack of mercy, military leaders, even believers, can easily turn a "just" war into an "unjust" one. Derek Kidner says that naming a child Jezreel "was like a politician naming his child Peterloo or Katyn or Soweto" (historical places of massacre).[7] This name would be a continual opportunity for the prophet to explain God's righteous anger. It was a name that had the fragrance of death and judgment. It had to be a frightening name for the unfaithful Israelites to continually hear, portending their own bloodbaths, and "scattering."

(Kathy) Let me help you understand this dry and clinically written paragraph that Dee just wrote. Have any of you seen the Ashley Judd movie *High Crimes*? Ashley plays an extremely competent lawyer who becomes passionate about defending her military husband; he has been accused of heading the massacre of innocent villagers in Vietnam. He proclaims his innocence throughout the movie, and she believes and trusts him the whole way. She lays her own reputation on the line to defend him. We find out at the end (not to ruin it for any of you) that this man she has so loved, who has been seemingly filled with honor and integrity, has been guilty and all about lies, hatred, and arrogance. Let's take artistic liberty and add to the story to help clarify what happened in Hosea. Imagine that this massacre took place in a village named Man Chu. Then suppose Ashley had been successful in defending her husband and *still* didn't know that he was guilty. Years go by, and she conceives their first child. She's a good Baptist girl (I'm really making this up now, but work with me), and one night as she's praying she asks God to give her a name for her baby. She hears a voice in the darkness. (Okay, well, maybe she's charismatic.) And God says, "His name shall be called Man

Chu." At that moment, deep in her spirit she knows that her husband is guilty of bloodshed and they will be reminded of the shame of his crime for the rest of their lives.

2. Explain why the Israelites would be uncomfortable with Hosea naming his son Jezreel.

   _____

   _____

   _____

3. The Israelites trusted in their military might. What would God therefore do, and where would he do it (Hosea 1:5)?

   _____

   _____

   _____

4. There are multiple meanings in the word *Jezreel,* for this word meaning "scatter" can also picture a farmer scattering seed and so means "sows or plants," as well. Eventually the land of death would become the land of life. Look ahead to Hosea 2:21–22 and describe the transformation that Hosea was able to see happening in the future.

   _____

   _____

   _____

5. The Lord's word can bring both fear and hope. How can you see both fear and hope in the word *Jezreel* in Hosea?

   _____

   _____

   _____

6. The paternity of the next two children was in doubt. What name did God instruct Hosea to give to the next child, a daughter? What does the name mean? What word was used specifically for Israel? What word was used specifically for Judah?

   _____

   _____

   _____

7. Imagine that the Lord spoke to you in a dream and told you He was no longer going to show you mercy. Then, night after night, in your dreams you saw a haunting figure wearing a sign that said No Mercy. How do you think you would feel and respond?

   _____

   _____

How frightening to lose the mercy of God! Yet, clearly, God's mercy has its limits. R. C. Sproul recalls being in seminary and preaching before his superiors. "I was so excited about God's mercy that in my enthusiasm I made reference to the infinite grace of God. After the sermon the first question that was raised was: 'Mr. Sproul, where did you ever get the idea that God's grace was infinite, that it had no boundaries, that there is no limit to His pity?'"[8]

God is not obligated to show mercy to any of us. Mercy, by its very definition, is undeserved grace. There are many warnings in Scripture, and one of them is right here: if we harden our hearts, we may not be able to hear the soft pleadings of the Spirit. God may indeed withdraw for a time. He is not obligated to continue to strive with the hard hearts of men. This is a stern warning we must not ignore.

8. Is there an area of your life where you have been hardening your heart to the Spirit of God? Where is it and why should you wake up?

   _____

   _____

   _____

> O my hearers, God is very gracious, but his Spirit shall not always strive with you. A little more sin, and you may be over the boundary, and God may give you up. Stay, I pray you! Do not further provoke. Repent, and turn unto the Lord with full purpose of heart.[9]

9. What was the name of the third child? What did it mean? Why was this the most frightening name of all?

   _____

   _____

   _____

This was the high point in God's judgment. God disowning His children? Could it be? What terror this name would inspire. You will see, as this portrait unfolds, that God never completely disowned them, but for a time He treated them as if they were not His. For a time He will not be the Great I AM to them. All of these names, Derek Kidner explains, are "shouts of warning, not irrevocable sentences."[10] When judgment and pain come into a believer's life, though it may indeed last a long time—even a lifetime—it is never the end of the story.

10. After the judgment and pain, what hope did God give in Hosea 2:21–23?

   _____

   _____

   _____

That is the story of all who have ever been saved: Scattered! Not-Pitied! Not-My-People! But now: Planted! Pitied! The People of God![11]

11. Take one of the children's names and both of its meanings, and tell what it means to you personally.

_____

_____

_____

Day 5

You Are the Potter

You may want to sing "Have Thine Own Way" and ask Him for strength to surrender to help you prepare for this lesson. Review your memory work and the week's study.

One weekend we were at an event where a potter made an urn on stage—a grand and beautiful piece like you might see at the entrance of a luxurious hotel in Paris. As he worked, he shared his testimony of how God had been continually molding him. We watched him transform a lump of clay before our very eyes. He turned it into a vessel of beauty with delicate etchings. Just as we were all ready to give him a standing ovation, he crushed it down, folding the top within, destroying what we thought was a masterpiece. We gasped. He reached into what was left of the urn, and explained that hidden within were ugly scraps of clay that he still had to remove. Just like Jesus, he began a good work and was intent on finishing it. When he finally finished his creation, it was glorious, lovelier than the earlier one he had crushed.

(*Kathy*) It struck me that each of us was clueless as to what he was creating. Before he even set foot onstage, he knew what the finished work would look like! That was so comforting to me, because there have been many times in God's molding my life I've wondered:

Where is He taking me?

What is happening?

Am I going to be okay?

And every time I look back, I've seen that He was intent on doing a good work in me. He brings beauty from ashes.

It should give us confidence that the same Lord who created this beautiful world out of nothing is at work conforming us to the image of Christ. Does He care? Is He just? Is He wise? Oh yes.

When we are unfaithful,
> *He is faithful.*

When we forget Him,
> *He remembers us.*

When we run away,

> *He pursues us.*

He has begun a good work in us, and the Word will bring it to completion, even if it means taking us through the fire.

I've sung songs with words such as "You are the Potter, and I am the clay," for years, but to actually see this man on stage as if he were in his workshop was life changing. He was Jesus, and the clay was me. Whenever I pictured a potter I thought of two hands delicately sculpting a piece of art. Fingers and hands would move with artistic, graceful precision. But as he molded the clay, it was much more involved than that. There was an intense and bold determination as he was hugging and holding the clay. His face never softened its concentration. He aggressively threw his whole body into the work, and yet, it was such a tender sight. There was a love in him for the piece he was creating. I almost felt as if I were being intrusive just to watch. Not only were his hands and arms covered with clay but, one side of his face got completely smeared. His cheek was helping to balance the object of his heart.

(Dee) To me, it almost reminded me of the act of making love: sometimes tender, sometimes intense, but totally encompassing, embracing, and loving. *Seeing* this helped me to realize that though being on the Potter's wheel can be painful, it is *always* good, for He truly loves us.

When we adopted our daughter Anne, our older daughter Sally went into a full-blown depression. At the time I wondered, *What have we done? Have we made a mistake?* We had a beautiful family. But it seemed it was crumbling before my eyes. I didn't have a vision for the future, but God did. And just like the potter we were watching, God was so close. Out of the intense heat and stretching, God removed things we hadn't even been able to see and built an even stronger and more loving family. Now, as we walk through Steve's cancer, there are many times when grief wells up in me, and I cannot imagine how I will survive. The heat seems too intense, the pain too sharp, the future too bleak. But when I remember that look of concentration and love in the potter's eyes, I can yield.

1. Read Isaiah 29:13–16.
   A. Describe how God saw His people (v. 13).

   _____

   _____

   B. Therefore, what did God say He was going to do (v. 14)?

   _____

   _____

What seems wonderful to the Lord may seem frightening to us. Here in Isaiah, God's people were going to face major purging and refining, but God could see the beautiful end result.

   C. What huge mistake about God were the people making (v. 15)?

   _____

   _____

D. Do you ever fall into the error of verses 13 or 15? Explain.

_____

_____

E. When we question God, what is that like (v. 16)?

_____

_____

2. Look back at a painful time in your life in which God fashioned character, wisdom, and beauty in you. What happened, and how did God bring out beauty in you from it?

_____

_____

_____

In the same way, the Israelites in Hosea's day were going to experience extreme pain. All would suffer enormously, and many would lose their lives, though all who believed would enter heaven. However, they themselves, if they survived, or their children had the hope of restoration and of becoming a much more beautiful vessel than they were before. God is intent upon refining His people.

3. In the following passages, describe the judgment and then the promise that Hosea prophesies:
A. The judgment: Hosea 1:4–5.

_____

_____

B. The promise: Hosea 2:21–23.

_____

_____

C. The judgment: Hosea 1:6.

_____

_____

D. The promise: Hosea 2:23.

_____

_____

E. The judgment: Hosea 1:9

_____

_____

F. The promise: Hosea 2:23

_____

_____

The Potter who changes the clay from a lump into a beautiful work of art is the Word who created man from the dust of the earth and is fashioning him and conforming him into the image of Christ. Essential to the process is water. As we watched a potter in action on stage, he kept cupping water with his hand to moisten the clay. How exciting it was to realize that the Word used *His* word to keep us pliable. How often do we say, "I'm so dry"? If we don't allow the Word to water us, He won't be able to accomplish His perfect will for us.

4. Memorization is one of the ways to keep the water flowing. When you memorize a passage, you can pray through it and meditate on it even when you are not sitting down with your Bible. If you have had some success in this area, share with the others how you do it and how it has blessed you. This will encourage them in the memory work of this study.

    _____

    _____

    _____

There is an important and, for some, a controversial theme thread throughout Scripture: we have freedom to make choices, but some areas God completely determines. We are a people who like always to be in control. When we hear that God may harden a heart or choose a people for Himself or put a righteous man over the fire, we may bristle and say, "That's not fair!" But Paul, in quoting Hosea in Romans 9, sternly rebuked that kind of arrogant thinking and asked, "Is there unrighteousness with God?" (Romans 9:21).

How can we argue with the wisdom of a holy God? We must humble ourselves before Him and realize that the God who made the universe is smarter than we are. Each of us deserves His wrath, but He has chosen, in His wisdom, to show mercy to whom He will show mercy. (It isn't just that I'm a Calvinist who feels deeply about this truth—that's what the passage says.)

When a loved one has cancer, God may allow Him to suffer and die, or He may spare him and heal him. When we sin and deserve the consequences, God may allow us to experience the great pain of those consequences, or He may have mercy and relent. Again, He is not obligated. He will show mercy to whom He will show mercy. He is good. He is just. And He will do all things well in His time.

5. In Hosea 1:6–7, to whom did the Lord say He would no longer have mercy? To whom did He say He would extend mercy?

    _____

    _____

    _____

The Lord makes distinctions among guilty men according to the sovereignty of his grace. "I will no more have mercy upon the house of Israel; but I will have mercy upon the house of Judah." Had not Judah sinned too? Might not the Lord have given up Judah also! Indeed he might justly have done so, but he delighteth in mercy. Many sin, and righteously bring upon themselves the punishment due to sin: they believe not in Christ, and die in their sins. But God has mercy, according to the greatness of his heart, upon multitudes who could not be saved on any other footing but that of undeserved mercy. Claiming his royal right he says, "I will have mercy on whom I will have mercy."[12]

6. Though it is difficult, it is important to realize that none of us deserves mercy. Jesus tried to turn the light on this hard truth with a parable. Read Matthew 20:1–16. Why were the workers who had worked all day angry? What principles were they missing according to verses 13–15?

_____

_____

_____

We cannot earn God's mercy. Most of us have come to understand this. We are saved only by His mercy, only by His grace. But when it comes to life, we may think that we can obligate God to do certain things for us. If we often work very hard, if we often abstain from sin, or if we often pray and fast, we may think He *must* heal us, or *must* give us a baby, or a position, or a house. Just as in salvation, so also in life—mercy is *His* to give, and He is not wrong to withhold it from anyone.

What moves the heart of God is not parading before Him our righteousness but crying out for mercy, remembering that He has purposes we cannot see. Paul addressed these hard passages from Hosea in Romans 9. This is an important but challenging passage, and we can only touch on it. For those who do wish to look at it more closely, we have a recommended resource.[13]

Read Romans 9:14–26.

7. Sometimes God gives a person over to himself, actually hardening an already hard heart, as He did in Romans 1. What example did Paul give in Romans 9:17, and for what purpose was the man's heart hardened?

_____

_____

_____

_____

8. When we question God's judgment, why do we have things upside down (Romans 9: 20–21)?

_____

_____

_____

9. Find a contrast for each of the following names in Romans 9:22–26:

A vessel of wrath /_____

Not My people /_____

Not beloved /_____

10. If God has shown mercy to you—if you are His child, His beloved—what should be your response?

_____

_____

_____

Review

How were you "kissed" by the King this week through His Word or His presence?

_____

_____

_____

Prayer Time

Cluster in small groups. Begin by thanking the Lord for some of His specific benefits. Then, if you are willing, lift up the need you expressed in day 4, question 8 and allow the others to support you.

The Brokenhearted Bridegroom
Artist: Martin French (www.martinfrench.com)

Week 5
THE BROKENHEARTED BRIDEGROOM

It is a bold and creative stroke by which God, instead of banning sexual imagery from religion, rescues and raises it to portray the ardent love and fidelity which are the essence of His covenant. Having made that clear, He can now go on to show what concord and delight the full flowering of that marriage God and man will bring.

—DEREK KIDNER[1]

MEMORY VERSE:
HOSEA 7:14A

*I*f you have experienced betrayal by a spouse, best friend, or close family member, then you know there is no pain like it. When you are knit together with someone, whether in body or in soul, and a severing occurs, it tears at your very being. You are unable to sleep, to concentrate, to keep the tears from flowing. You keep thinking, *How could they do this after I have loved them so well and so long? I would have laid down my life for them—and now, this?*

(*Dee*) When I was a little girl, a very pleasant woman came to our house every Friday to do our ironing. Mrs. Hahn sang as she ironed, or listened with a smile to my childish chatter. I remember visiting her at her simple home. Money was tight for her family and her husband's job required him to be away a great deal, but she had made it a little piece of heaven, complete with ruffled curtains, candles, and the fragrance of homemade bread. She spoke lovingly of her husband, and it seemed an ideal marriage.

But when he died, we discovered that, for forty years, he had lived a double life—he had a wife and children in another state. The money Mrs. Hahn had taken home from ironing, he had spent on another family. The nights she had given up with him, he had given to another. The covenant she had honored, he had trampled upon. When she discovered his lifelong treachery, it was as if her kite, which once soared, took a sudden dive.

She still came to our home, but she no longer sang or smiled or listened attentively to my chatter. When I think about how she must have felt, I can better understand the emotion and contradicting statements in Hosea. I can picture Mrs. Hahn thinking, after she discovered her husband's infidelity, *I was not his wife, and he was not my husband!* And yet, she *was* his wife, and he *was* her husband. Mrs. Hahn helps me understand the statements in Hosea, when God accused His bride in court and cried,

Rebuke your mother, rebuke her,
for she is not my wife,
and I am not her husband. (Hosea 2:2)

Of course we are His wife, and He is our Husband, but, oh, how the love can go out of our relationship because of our infidelities. It is also important to see that it is here, when the Lord said, "I am not her husband," that He was saying, "For a time, I will not be the Great I AM to my people."

It may seem odd, as Max Lucado writes, "to think of God as an enthralled lover . . . as a suitor intoxicated on love."[2] Yet that is how He painted Himself in Hosea, as a Bridegroom whose heart was broken.

So many of you have written to tell us how your lives have been transformed by the Falling in Love with Jesus series. Yet a few have wondered about approaching Jesus as Bridegroom. Even though God Himself does it, we understand how strange it may seem to use romantic or sexual imagery in regard to our relationship with God. It is vital we take the time to address these concerns right away, in our first day this week.

VIDEO NOTES FOR WEEK 5

Watch the video first, and then put your chairs in a circle to discuss this lesson. Don't cover the following questions in discussion.

1. Is the portrait of Jesus as our Bridegroom scriptural?

    _____

    _____

    _____

2. The sexual connotation can be distorted when we neglect the poetic genre of Scripture. For example:

    Prose is a matter of _____ account.

    Poetry focuses on _____.

    Prose is directed to the mind, poetry to the _____.

    Both are true.

3. Derek Kidner writes, "It is a bold and creative stroke by which God, instead of_____ sexual imagery from religion, rescues and raises it to portray the ardent love and_____ which are the essence of His covenant."[3]

4. Poetry has great value because

    _____

    _____

    _____

5. Isn't the bride simply the corporate bride—all of God's people—and not the individual? The book of Ephesians gives three pictures of God's people, all beginning with B:

The b_____,

the b_____,

and the b_____.

	Individual	Corporate
The Building	You, as an individual are God's temple, so flee sexual immorality. (1 Corinthians 6:18–19)	Together we are built up into God's temple and Christ is head. (Ephesians 1:22; 2:21)
The Body	Each member is valuable. (1 Corinthians 12:18–25)	Many members, yet one body. (1 Corinthians 12:20)
The Bride	Addressed to individual, "Let him kiss me." (Song of Solomon 1:2)	Addressed to corporate Bride (Revelation 19:6–9)

6. What is the main message we should gain from Jesus as our Bridegroom?

We are in a _____ relationship with Jesus. He wants the r_____ of a beautiful m_____ in our lives.

Religious syncretism is the _____ and _____ of belief systems.

7. What are some things that might be taken away from you if you choose to move out from God's covering?

_____

_____

_____

As our Bridegroom, Jesus woos, wins, and weds. If you've come to know Jesus, you know He initially wooed you. Because Jesus continually is drawing us close to His heart, share a way He has drawn you to Himself recently. (You were broken during a worship song, you experienced sweet fellowship with someone because of Jesus, you saw a beautiful sunset and were reminded of His majesty.)

What do you particularly remember from the video? Why?

INTRODUCTION QUESTIONS

Please cover these questions in your discussion group. They are vital.

1. In what ways can a spouse's infidelity and abandonment be even more painful than being widowed?

   _____

   _____

   _____

2. How does Mrs. Hahn's story shed light on the Lord's statement about His people: "She is not my wife, and I am not her husband"?

   _____

   _____

   _____

3. Has God banned sexual imagery from the Bible? If not, what has He done?

   _____

   _____

   _____

Day 1

Jesus, Lover of My Soul

Other than the portrait of God as our Father, the portrait of Jesus as our Bridegroom is one writers of the Old and New Testaments painted more frequently than any other. The Song of Songs used the analogy to show us the Lord's tenderness toward us. Hosea used the analogy to show us the Lord's broken heart. Isaiah and Jeremiah are filled with pictures of our Bridegroom and of us, often as an unfaithful bride. Hidden in Psalm 45, the book of Ruth, and many other passages is Jesus, our

Kinsman-Redeemer Husband, our royal Bridegroom. Jesus told not one, but many parables about a bridegroom, a great wedding feast, and virgins who were not permitted to come to the wedding feast. Paul told us that earthly marriages are a picture of a much deeper reality, the mystery of the relationship of Christ with His bride, the church.

The Bridegroom analogy is important. As Jack Deere has said, "The greatest danger to the church today is not from without, but from within."[3] Our greatest danger is losing our passion and turning Christianity into ritual instead of the love relationship God intended it to be.

Doctrine is important, but doctrine without love is legalism, just as love without doctrine is license. God's heart is for truth, but not truth without devotion. God is looking for true worshipers who will keep a covenant relationship with Him. He rejoices over us, and it breaks His heart to be forgotten, to see us running after other lovers, reducing our relationship to ritual, breaking our "marriage vows."

Yet still, many have struggled with the whole analogy and have asked good questions. We'd like to address these questions now.

Isn't there a sexual connotation to the bridegroom analogy that is inappropriate?

Anytime a portrait is given to help us understand a holy God, it is possible to press certain aspects too far, distorting the meaning. Because we've talked about intimacy with God in this series, it has sometimes broken our hearts that some have been able to equate deep intimacy only with sex. God *does* use sexual images to convey a point, for after all, He created sex, but it is always in the purest and holiest sense. He desires oneness with us. He has made a covenant with us. He has betrothed us to Himself. In Hosea, He says,

> *I will betroth you to Me in faithfulness,*
> *And you shall know the LORD.* (Hosea 2:20)

Derek Kidner's comment is worth repeating:

> It is a bold and creative stroke by which God, instead of banning sexual imagery from religion, rescues and raises it to portray the ardent love and fidelity which are the essence of His covenant.[4]

If we have a quarrel with using sexual imagery to portray our relationship with the Lord, our quarrel must be with the Lord Himself, for it is found throughout Scripture. We will give you a few such examples.

1. Explain the point the Lord is making through each of the following sexual analogies:
   A. Jeremiah 3:1–2

   _____

   _____

B. Hosea 2:5

_____

_____

C. 2 Corinthians 11:2

_____

_____

The Scripture also uses figures of intimacy in a positive way. The Song of Songs is filled with the bride's longing for greater intimacy with her bridegroom. When she says, for example, "Let him kiss me with the kisses of his mouth" (Song of Songs 1:2), this isn't a literal kiss from Jesus (must we even say it?), but a metaphorical one. Tremper Longman III, professor of biblical studies at Westmont, writes,

> Most debates over the interpretation of Scripture are really debates over the identification of a text's genre.[5]

For example, the genre of poetry is very different from the genre of prose. We can take prose very literally, but poetry speaks in metaphors. When the Psalms tell us we can find shelter under the shadow of God's wings, we are to apply it metaphorically. When the Song of Songs talks about the Lord kissing us, it is metaphorical.

(_Dee_) Recently a woman who was seeking truth but was in a church that questions the validity of the Scriptures said to me, "The Bible says the earth is flat."

I said, "Actually, Job, one of the earliest books, says the earth is a sphere. Where did you get the idea the Bible said the earth was flat?"

She said, "Well, our minister told us it says that 'His voice goes to the end of the earth.'"

I shook my head, angry that someone was using the metaphorical phrase to support the untrue claim that the Bible is in error.

The sexual images are definitely metaphorical, but they have a point. If you are watching the video, Kathy sings a song that she wrote as a new Christian, based on the romantic images from the Song of Songs. Somehow the Spirit of God helped her then to understand the main point of this book: God longs for relationship with us, to walk with us, to "hold" us, to have us sit under His shadow contentedly. How we need to approach our relationship with Him longing for His touch, instead of simply as a duty!

2. Look at the following passages that describe a similar truth. In each case, explain the truth expressed and then note whether the genre is poetry or prose.
   A. Exodus 14:27–28

   _____

   _____

   Exodus 15:10

   _____

   _____

B. Song of Solomon 1:2

_____

_____

Psalm 84:1–2

_____

_____

C. Exodus 20:3

_____

_____

Hosea 2:2–5

_____

_____

3. What are the advantages of the poetic genre? of the prose genre?

_____

_____

_____

We are not to press metaphors too hard but to look for the central truth. They speak to the head through the heart, impacting with memorable emotion. Another reason believers may struggle with sexual imagery is due to the way our world has polluted the beauty of the marriage bed. Sexual immorality is rampant, and images of impurity flow, like a sewer, into our minds and hearts. And yet the holiness of the sexual union between a husband and wife has not changed.

4. What does Hebrews 13:4 say about the marriage bed?

_____

_____

_____

5. What parallel does Scripture make in Ephesians 5:30–33?

_____

_____

_____

_____

(_Kathy_) Even as a single woman I understand the portrait. I may not have a husband, but I am living in the "deeper reality." I am the bride of Christ. I do not have an earthly sexual partner, but just as married women can understand the spiritual analogy, so can I. That is such a joy to me, knowing I am in covenant with the living God. Jesus meets the deepest needs of my soul and tenderly directs me through this life.

Jesus, the Word, often spoke in metaphors. When He wept over Jerusalem, saying He wished He could gather her as a mother hen gathers her chicks under her wings, we know He was speaking metaphorically. The Word likes to paint pictures to penetrate the heart. Just how far can we press the pictures of a wedding feast, a Bridegroom coming on a white horse for His bride, or of the Lord rejoicing over us with singing? The evidence seems strong that it is more than a metaphor, and yet, it is a mystery. Read carefully what Paul wrote about this picture:

> *"For this reason a man will leave his father and mother and be united to his wife, and*
> *the two will become one flesh." This is a profound mystery—but I am talking about*
> *Christ and the church.* (Ephesians 5:31–32 NIV)

We understand that not everyone is going to be comfortable with the portrait of Jesus as Bridegroom, just as not everyone is comfortable with the portrait of God as Father. We tend to process spiritual things by our human experiences. If we have had negative earthly role models or painful experiences, the Lord as Husband or as Father may be difficult for us. But God is so good. In the process of our growing in relationship with Him, healing starts to happen, and we relate to God in ways He has so desired. In fact, one day the portrait we pushed away may become the most meaningful one of all. In the meantime, let us give one another grace, as we all are at different points in our journey to the high places.

There's another question that we hear occasionally:

Isn't the picture of the bride just for the whole church, the corporate body—and not for us as individuals?

There are three clear pictures in Ephesians (and throughout Scripture) to describe the body of believers: a building, a body, and a bride. In each, there is an individual and a corporate application. It is important that we see both. For example, if you consider the picture of the body, the hand by itself is very important and certainly would be missed were it cut off. The hand should consider itself valuable. Yet the hand should never say, "I do not need the eye!" The hand must see the importance of working together with the whole body.

Likewise, the picture of the bride is individual but also corporate. Dee's pastor, Mike Lano, said, "How else can you interpret the Song of Solomon *except* on an individual level? Yet it is also vital that we see the bride corporately and realize how beautiful we are to the Lord when we are all in harmony. We must see both the individual and corporate application in all three metaphors." (Refer to the chart on page 81 to discover the answers to the following questions.)

6. The Building
    A. Read 1 Corinthians 6:18–19. What does it say, what does it mean, and how would you apply it? Do you think this is an individual or corporate application?

    _____

    _____

B. Read Ephesians 1:22; 2:19–22. What does it say, what does it mean, and how would you apply it? Do you think this is an individual or corporate application?

_____

_____

7. The Body
   A. Read 1 Corinthians 12:15–25. What does it say, what does it mean, and how would you apply it? Do you think this is an individual or corporate application?

   _____

   _____

   B. Read 1 Corinthians 12:12–14; 20. What does it say, what does it mean, and how would you apply it? Do you think this is an individual or corporate application?

   _____

   _____

8. The Bride
   A. Read the Song of Solomon 1:2; 2:16a. What does it say, what does it mean, and how would you apply it? Do you think this is an individual or corporate picture?

   _____

   _____

   B. Read Revelation 19:9; 21:1–2. What does it say, what does it mean, and how would you apply it? Do you think this is an individual or corporate picture?

   _____

   _____

The building, the body, and the bride all have individual and corporate applications. However, even when a writer in Scripture addresses the church, there is always an individual application. It would be a great evasion to say, "God isn't asking me, personally, to be faithful—this message is for the church." When John wrote, "God so loved the world," it didn't mean that God didn't love us as individuals. God is so personal that He knows our names, the number of hairs on our heads, and our innermost thoughts. When He tells us He loves us, when He tells us He wants us to be faithful, He is talking to us as individuals, who make up the entire body of believers.

Yet in emphasizing the individual aspect of this picture, it is easy to fall into the other error: neglecting the corporate picture. One young woman wisely observed, "So often women have a tendency not to get along with other women—to feel intimidated, to be easily hurt, to be jealous—so they withdraw from their responsibility to the body of Christ. Since Christ is preparing a bride that is to be without spot or wrinkle, the goal is for the _whole_ bride to be that way." Another woman observed, "Sometimes individuals will not see the need to be involved in godly community and the local church. They fail to see that this is a primary way the Lord has provided for them. They'll justify their lack of involvement by emphasizing that they don't need church to love God: 'I'm okay. Jesus is with me.'"

While the picture of *The Bridegroom* may be particularly meaningful to us as individuals, and particularly to us as women, it is vital to remember the corporate aspect. The bride of Christ is made up of all believers: Jews, Gentiles, singles, marrieds, men, women, and children. There is a beauty in corporate worship, for example, that we cannot achieve alone. There is a beauty in loving one another that we cannot achieve alone. There is a beauty in sharpening one another, in holding one another accountable, in praying for and supporting one another, in coming under the protection of a local church, that we cannot achieve alone. If we are not actively involved in the body of Christ, then we are *not* a beautiful bride.

When John saw "the Holy City, the New Jerusalem, coming down out of heaven from God, prepared as a bride beautifully dressed for her husband" (Revelation 21:2 NIV), he was seeing the *entire* bride of Christ, in all her many-faceted colors, made up of every tribe and nation, loving one another in holy harmony.

We understand the injustices and hurts that many have experienced with Christians. You can really get to the point where you don't want anything to do with them. But no matter how hypocritical, sick, or healthy the body of Christ has been through the ages, it is *still* and always will be His body, His building, and His bride—and the gates of hell will not prevail against it. Scripture is clear that we need each other and that forsaking being together grieves and angers the Lord.

9. How are you involved with other believers? Are you actively involved in a healthy church? (We'll look at signs of a healthy church later in this lesson.) If not, what steps will you take to change that?

_____

_____

_____

Day 2
In Christ Alone

A song that might prepare your heart is the hymn "The Solid Rock."

Begin learning your memory passages. They are vivid word pictures, so though there are three, they shouldn't be too difficult.

The scene in Hosea 2 is a divorce court!

> *Put your mother on trial, plead with her!*
> *(For she is no wife of mine and I am not her husband.)*
> *Tell her to wash the paint from her face,*
> *And the seductions from between her breasts.* (Hosea 2:2 PHILLIPS)

R. C. Sproul says, "You can almost hear Hosea thinking, *God, how can You say, 'I'm going to divorce my people'? . . . You betrothed Yourself to these people forever. . . . It was a 'to death do us part.' . . . How can you even think about divorce even with the apostasy of the nation?*" So what is God saying? Sproul says God cries, "I'm saying both! You are not my people, and yet, still [and you sense the anguish, how He cannot let her go] you *are* my people."[6] Derek Kidner sees it like this: "God is not saying that He is going back on His marriage covenant, for the whole thrust of Hosea is that God will not go back on His marriage vows. What He is saying instead is, 'The reality has gone out of our relationship.'"[7] Sometimes the brokenhearted Bridegroom weeps, sometimes He rages. Nothing seems to trouble the Lord more than being forgotten and betrayed by the one for whom He has sacrificed so much.

1. The Lord used the very words of His bride to accuse her in court. What were they (Hosea 2:5)?

    _____

    _____

    _____

2. Describe what a marriage might look like when "the reality has gone out of the relationship."

    _____

    _____

    _____

3. Is the "reality" still in your marriage with the Lord, or is it a marriage in name only, for the sake of appearances? Give evidence for your answer.

    _____

    _____

    _____

What were the "other lovers" His people were running after? Israel committed the age-old sin of syncretism (mixing and merging of religions). While she (His bride) claimed to worship the Lord, there were other gods "in her bed," for she also worshiped Baal and the gods of the culture around her.

There is more to Hosea 2:5 than might at first be apparent. The gods of Canaan, such as Baal, were largely patrons of fertility. To get the best results from these gods or "husbands," as they were sometimes called, the people performed sexual acts in the temple, thinking this inspired these gods to give them fertility in their herds and crops. The people felt that the God of Abraham, Isaac, and Jacob was somehow out of His element, so they had to turn to less noble gods, and those gods became addictive. Derek Kidner explains,

> There was the fascination of the forbidden and decadent—the exciting exchange of Yahweh's broad daylight for the twilight world of violent gods, with their raw passions, cruelties, and ecstasies; an exchange which has a perennial appeal.[8]

We've seen, as Derek Kidner says, "a modern dethroning of God" in today's church. In certain issues of today's culture, Yahweh seems to be somewhat out of His realm. It's almost as if we say, "Yes, I understand that God is omnipotent, omnipresent, and omniscient, but . . ." Throughout the history of the church, His people have often felt that God wasn't quite enough. We can tend to get a "faith in Jesus, plus that too (a god that will really help us!)" mentality. Mixing in "other gods," whether they are other religions or the occult, is syncretism. As Kidner says,

> These beliefs are not as foreign or remote from our age as they might seem. The idea that God has little relevance to the natural world is taken for granted by the secularized majority.[9]

In Hosea's day, they turned to violent gods. Christians who want to lose weight or stop smoking have turned to hypnotists. People may say they trust Jesus, but then, because He isn't telling them all they want to know about the future, turn to astrology or mysticism. There is the feeling: *I need a little more help here.* Saul did it when he wasn't hearing from God by going to the witch of Endor, and people who call themselves "believers" may fall prey to the occult when they feel God isn't giving them the help they need.

Many individuals belong to Bible-believing churches yet are also full-standing members of secret societies such as the Freemasons. Freemasonry *is* a religion whose tenets are in opposition to Christianity. While Freemasonry itself is syncretism, and its beliefs vary from country to country, its proponents do agree that man is not sinful.[10] Therefore there is no need for a Savior. You get to heaven through good works that will lead you to the "Grand Lodge on High."[11] How can you embrace both Christianity and Freemasonry? You cannot, though many individuals say they can, and that there is no conflict.

(Dee) One year a well-known New Age speaker was scheduled to speak at a women's retreat at a mainline denomination in Lincoln, Nebraska. The day before the event she became very ill. The coordinator called me in a panic and said, "This woman was going to take us higher—do you think you could do that for us?"

I said, "I certainly know the God who can."

When I spoke, I shared how Jesus had changed my life and I presented the gospel clearly. As soon as I named Jesus, some looked down, studying the carpet, but others had faces full of longing, eager to embrace the truth. Afterward, I read their church bulletin, describing their choice of Sunday school classes. They offered some good Bible studies with materials from Max Lucado and Chuck Swindoll. But they also offered New Age classes, mysticism, and yoga. Just as in Hosea's day, these people who claimed the name of the one true God had other "gods" in their bed. This is religious syncretism.

4. How have you seen syncretism (the mixing of Christianity with other religions) in the lives of individual believers or in some churches?

_____

_____

_____

The Lord was making a parallel here with earthly marriage. Jesus said that a legitimate ground for divorce was adultery. However, even though Israel has committed "adultery" by going to other gods, and she was in court facing her Husband's accusations, His goal was repentance, not a permanent severing of the marriage.

5. A divorce is not legal unless there is a certificate of divorce. With that in mind, in Isaiah 50:1, what question did God ask of Israel? What was the implicit answer? What was the second preposterous question?

   _____

   _____

   _____

God will never sell His bride to pay His bills. He will never divorce her, breaking His covenant. But He *may* separate from her for a time. Separation, as painful as it is, can be tough love for the wronged spouse. We see this in earthly marriages. It is hard to separate from someone you love, even if that person is being unfaithful or has an addiction that is destroying both of you. But often the only hope for healing *is* in separation, and in insisting that the wayward spouse get help and bear the fruit of repentance before you take him back.

True love is sacrificial. On a spiritual level, God didn't want to give Israel up, even for a time, but He had to, to bring her to her senses. He was willing to bring the law down on her, even to the point of exposing her hidden sins so that she would give up her destructive behavior. In Scripture, we see God withdrawing and being silent when His people have been unfaithful to Him.

This was a kind of "separation" from His "wife." But God's people had His promise of full reconciliation one day. For a time the marriage seemed over, yet God's intent was never divorce but repentance.

6. What evidence of genuine repentance from Israel did God ask for in Hosea 2:2?

   _____

   _____

   _____

Day 3
He Who Began a Good Work in Me

Be still before Him for five minutes. Then sing to Him. Learn your memory passages.

Some husbands, when their brides are unfaithful, will simply put up with it, for they fear losing them completely. (The same is true with women when their husbands are unfaithful.) But the Lord demands faithfulness. If His people would not repent, He would find ways to help her.

1. What was our Bridegroom's first strategy, according to Hosea 2:6–8? What did He hope would be the result?

_____

_____

_____

2. What does Proverbs 22:5 teach about thorns?

_____

_____

_____

3. In the story of the prodigal son, God began to block him in "with thorns." How did He do that, according to Luke 15:14–16?

_____

_____

_____

4. How then did the prodigal respond (Luke 15:17–19)?

_____

_____

_____

5. How is this similar to Hosea 2:6–7?

_____

_____

_____

6. On the basis of all of these passages, what do you think a "hedge of thorns" represents?

_____

_____

_____

If thorns will not block our determined pursuit of false lovers, our Bridegroom has a second strategy. After the hedge of thorns, He may build a wall, a sweet protection shielding us from temptation and trial.

7. What had irritated Satan, according to Job 1:9–10?

_____

_____

_____

In the Lord's Prayer we are told to pray, "Lead me not into temptation." We know God does not tempt (see James 1:13), so what does this mean? The Greek word for *temptation* can also be translated "trial." We can and should pray that God will either not lead us into trial, or, if for our best He chooses to, that He will give us the strength to give Him glory in it.

8. Can you think of areas in your life where you feel the Lord has protected you or strengthened you in a trial?

_____

_____

_____

(Kathy) Many times I've gotten a morning phone call from a dear friend like this: ""Kath, I was up in the middle of the night, just really disturbed in my spirit. I prayed for you for quite some time. Are you okay? I feel as if something or someone is trying to bring you down. It feels dangerous. Maybe you can pray about it, because if it is God telling me this, it might save you from a lot of trouble and turmoil."

9. Read Hosea 2:9–12. Describe the Lord's strategy to help His unfaithful bride reconsider. Be specific.

_____

_____

_____

Sometimes the very things that once gave us joy can turn to gravel in our mouths. In Hosea, Israel's parties became like wakes. The vineyards that fed them became forests, hiding wild animals that would devour them.

10. Have you ever experienced something sinful that you enjoyed actually turning and becoming terrible to you? If so, share.

_____

_____

_____

11. What is the closing cry of the Lord in Hosea 2:13? Why was this the primary sin?

_____

_____

_____

Many of the pictures in Hosea are also in Ezekiel 16:1–43. In this parable Ezekiel compared Jerusalem to a baby, then to a bride, and finally, after the Lord richly blessed them, a harlot.

Remember, the Word paints pictures in order to help us understand His heart. We pray you will immerse yourself in these pictures to understand God's love for you.

12. Read Ezekiel 16:1–7.

   A. In verses 4–5, describe the picture given of God's people, and therefore, of each individual believer.

   _____

   _____

   B. What did the Lord speak in verse 6, and what was the result, according to verse 7?

   _____

   _____

   C. Find details in this picture that illustrate our great need for the Lord and His power to help us.

   _____

   _____

13. Describe the next picture in Ezekiel 16:8. What need of ours did Ezekiel present, and how did the Lord respond to that need?

   _____

   _____

   _____

The concept of the Lord's "covering" us is throughout Scripture. Sometimes the word is translated "covering," sometimes "wing," or sometimes "garment" (see Ruth 2:12, 3:9; Psalm 91:4). As our Husband, He covers us with provision and protection. A contrast to the loving protection of our heavenly Husband appears in Malachi 2:13–16, when men had cast their wives aside, failing to "cover" them. Their goal was to marry pagan women. Instead of covering their brides with protection and provision, they had treated them "treacherously." Their treachery was double, because they also failed to give their abandoned wives certificates of divorce, so the women were still bound, not free to remarry and be "covered" by another. In Malachi's day, it meant that women had either to beg or become prostitutes to survive. God's anger thundered at the husbands who had so abused the "wives of their youth." God will never be that kind of a husband to us.

14. From Ezekiel 16:15–34, describe some of the ways the unfaithful bride treated her Husband. Look for details.

   _____

   _____

   _____

15. In Ezekiel 16:35–39, what judgment would come to the unfaithful bride? What would happen to her "covering"?

_____

_____

_____

There are many parallels in this scene to the "divorce court" in Hosea. The sin was spiritual adultery, and the provisions God had given to His "wife," she had given to her lovers. He was going to rip His "covering" from her, exposing her nakedness (her sin) before her lovers. However, this was not the end of the story, for God would restore His bride to Himself and cover her again.

16. What emotions do you see on the part of the Lord in Ezekiel 16 that you also see in Hosea? Does it seem strange to you to think of God's being brokenhearted over our unfaithfulness? Why or why not?

_____

_____

_____

17. Has God ever taken His covering from you, exposing your sin to bring you to repentance?

_____

_____

_____

Day 4

I Have Betrothed You to One Husband

Sing "Open the Eyes of My Heart."

Review your memory work.

Not only did Hosea picture the longing that God had for a pure bride, but so also did John's gospel. We see it in the figure of John the Baptist, who called himself "the friend of the bridegroom" (John 3:29). You may be surprised at the Jewish wedding customs that called for a "friend of the bridegroom," but we believe you will also find them profoundly intriguing.

The "friend of the bridegroom" had several responsibilities. The first was to assure that the wedding hut or bridal chamber was in order. Then, after the bride and groom were carried up in the air, with joy and singing to this hut, the "friend of the bridegroom" waited outside for the bridegroom to call him and tell him to take the blood-stained cloth that was proof of the bride's virginity.[12] Finally, if, after the marriage, there were problems between the husband and wife, he was to act as a counselor.[13]

John Calvin saw all ministers of the gospel as "friends of the Bridegroom" who help assure the purity and fidelity of the bride and the health of her marriage to the Bridegroom.[14]

1. Read Deuteronomy 22:13–21.
   A. What protection did the bloodstained cloth give to a woman unjustly accused, according to verses 15–19?

   _____

   _____

   B. What happened to the woman who could not give evidence of her virginity (vv. 20–21)?

   _____

   _____

If you continue reading in Deuteronomy, you will see that God expected sexual morality on the part of the man as well. In the spiritual parallel, the concern is always the bride because Christ's purity is certain.

"Friends of the Bridegroom," or ministers of the gospel, must be vigilant about the purity of the bride. In the early church, false teachers tried to lead the Christians astray.

2. How did John the Baptist describe himself in John 3:28–30?

   _____

   _____

   _____

   _____

3. Think about John the Baptist's ministry. How did he help assure the purity of the bride? Consider the following passages:
   A. Matthew 3:1–6

   _____

   _____

   B. Matthew 3:7–12

   _____

   _____

   C. Matthew 14:3–4

   _____

   _____

4. Read 2 Corinthians 11:1–4.
   A. What picture did Paul use to describe his responsibility (v. 2)?

   _____

   _____

B. What was his fear and why (v. 3)?

_____

_____

C. What are the three different ways we might be corrupted (v. 4)?

_____

_____

One of the purposes of a local church is to guard the purity of the bride. Look for these signs of health when choosing a church:

- Sermons expound the Word of God and are truly like the voice of God to the congregation.

- Sermons are not primarily topical or political, but the pastor "preaches through" whole books, and you need your Bible to follow along.

- The integrity of the pastor is evident so that the message has credibility.

- Materials for teaching and the teachers themselves expound on Scripture and are under the authority of the elders.

- When members persist in open sin, the church practices discipline.

- The people take membership seriously, understanding their need to put themselves under the authority of a local body.

- The people are unified.

5. Are you a member of a local church that guards the purity of the bride? If not, other than God, to whom are you truly accountable?

_____

_____

_____

Day 5
The Wedding at Cana

Sing as the bride you are to your Bridegroom.

Review your memory work.

To the consternation of all good teetotalers, and even to those who occasionally have a glass of wine at dinner, it seems a strange first miracle. Wouldn't it have been more fitting for the Messiah to begin by giving sight to a blind man? Or by raising a dead man? But turning water into wine? How odd.

And yet, in the context of what we have just studied in Hosea, it makes perfect sense. Let's set the scene.

Life in the days of Jesus was hard; men and women alike labored from dawn until dusk with little relief, day after day. How they looked forward to the festivals—and oh, to the weddings! Philip Yancey tells us to picture happy scenes from *Fiddler on the Roof:*

> Peasant Jewish families dancing across the courtyard in their finest embroidered clothes, [scenes] of music and laughter, of banquet tables laden with clay platters of food and jugs of wine. The feast might go on for as long as a week, as long as the food and wine and good cheer held out. Truly a wedding was a time of high joy.[15]

It's natural to wonder about this wedding, this wine, this wonderful but rather strange first miracle. What does it all mean?

There have been many speculations. Wine often symbolizes the Holy Spirit. It is also true that just as a wedding broke through a bleak existence, so did the entrance of Jesus on the scene. Perhaps His beginning this new era at a wedding was appropriate, for He would end that era at His own wedding feast. Even at the Last Supper, and evermore, wine represented the blood of Christ.

(*Kathy*) How interesting it is to really look at the fact that Jesus used water and wine. There is so much symbolism there. When Jesus talked to Nicodemus, He told him he had to be born again (see John 3). He went on to say that Nicodemus was born of water (he'd had a natural birth), but he needed to be born of the Spirit to have a spiritual birth to be a new creation in Jesus. You cannot help but wonder if turning water into wine at the wedding foreshadowed the explanation of natural and spiritual births. John did not interpret this miracle, as he did most of the others, so we cannot know for certain.

Darrell Bock explains that a wedding signals a new era, with new relationships, new customs, and a new way of life. One of the primary themes in chapters 2–4 of John is "the replacement of Jewish institutions and religious views." For example, in John 4, the woman at the well asked Jesus if the correct place of worship was the temple in Jerusalem. Jesus told her that a change had come. Bock explains, "Jesus is the real temple; the Spirit he gives will replace the necessity of worshiping at Jerusalem."[16] Likewise, Jesus Himself, the Bread of Life, replaced the manna that God provided for the Israelites in the desert. Instead of a rain-making ceremony, Jesus would supply the living water; instead of the illumination in the temple court, Jesus was the Light of the World. With that as a context, turning the water into wine suddenly begins to make sense.

1. On the basis of the Scripture below, show how Jesus was the fulfillment or the replacement for the old.

A. The Law of Moses made way for (John 1:17):

_____

_____

B. The Passover lamb made way for (John 1:29):

_____

_____

C. The water from Jacob's well made way for (John 4:14):

_____

_____

D. Worshiping at the temple in Jerusalem made way for (John 4:21–24):

_____

_____

E. The manna in the wilderness made way for (John 6:35):

_____

_____

In the same way, those huge (twenty- to thirty-gallon) water jars, used for the ritual of ceremonial washing, were about to be transformed into containers of wine! Philip Yancey puts it like this:

> Even a wedding feast had to honor the burdensome rituals of cleansing. Jesus, perhaps with a twinkle in his eye, transformed those jugs, ponderous symbols of the old way, into wineskins, harbingers of the new. From purified water of the Pharisees came the choice new wine of a whole new era. The time for ritual cleansing had passed, the time for celebration had begun.[17]

Bock explains, "Weddings were not simply significant personal events in the ancient world, they also carried important symbolism (Hosea 2:14-23; 14:7 . . .). So when John calls this miracle a sign in 2:11, it pushes John's reader to see Jesus in these terms. The better wine comes later, after the earlier wine."[18]

Instead of the man-made rituals the religious leaders developed, God is looking for true worship. Instead of our trying and failing to keep the law, it is time for a whole new relationship, a love relationship! The Bridegroom will impart devotion to His bride, will give her a heart of flesh, will turn the water into wine!

2. Read John 2:1–12 and describe
   A. The water pots and their purpose (v. 6):

_____

_____

B. What Jesus told the servants to do (vv. 7–8):

_____

_____

C. What the master of the feast said (v. 10):

_____

_____

The synoptic (Matthew, Mark, and Luke) Gospels all refer to another incident that has important parallels to this incident in John. Jesus called Himself "the bridegroom," and talked about "old and new wine." To understand the incident, it is important to first understand the context. The Pharisees and religious leaders, full of pride and ignorant of their need for repentance, questioned Jesus's piety. Not only did Jesus and His disciples neglect their elaborate (and man-made) hand-washing ceremonies, but also their elaborate (and often man-made) traditions of fasting. (Jesus did fast, but not according to man-made tradition or to display piety. Fasting, within Judaism, had become corrupted.)

It is important to see that Jesus was taking a stand, not against true religion, but against corrupted religion. The thrust was similar to that of Hosea, where the religious leaders, in their practice of syncretism, had adulterated true worship.

3. Read Luke 5:27–39.
   A. What criticisms did the Pharisees have of Jesus and His disciples in Luke 5:30?

   _____

   _____

   B. What satirical comment did Jesus make in Luke 5:31? What did He mean?

   _____

   _____

   C. What was the Pharisees' next criticism in Luke 5:33?

   _____

   _____

   D. How did Jesus respond? Why was it not an appropriate time for fasting? When would it be?

   _____

   _____

   E. Two analogies illustrate the danger of mixing the old (the man-made traditions of the Pharisees) with the new (true worship). What was the first, according to Luke 5:36?

   _____

   _____

It is important to see that there was a tear that needed mending: "The point is that Jewish practice . . . has a rip and needs repair. The repair requires something fresh, not mere patchwork."[19] So often the church, His bride, has a tear that needs mending. That will keep on happening because we are still flesh and blood. Unfortunately we may fall prey to self-pity, thinking, *God hasn't met my need;* then we end up not even going to Him when we are in desperate need of a fresh wave of the Holy Spirit.

F. In the second analogy of the wineskins, it is helpful to know that when new wine ferments, it increases in volume. Describe the destruction that occurred when new wine was put into old wineskins (Luke 5:37).

_____

_____

This is the same kind of syncretism that made God so angry in Hosea's day. The Spirit of God is looking for true worshipers. Darrell Bock writes:

> The impossibility of a syncretistic approach to traditional Judaism and the new way is highlighted. . . . What Jesus offers is not mixable, even with a venerable faith like Judaism. . . . You cannot put something new on top of something old.[20]

G. What did the "new wine," the Spirit that Jesus gave, need? Why? (see Luke 5:38)

_____

_____

H. What satirical comment did Jesus make in Luke 5:39? (It is directed to the Pharisees and is similar to the satire in Luke 5:31.)

_____

_____

Jesus could see the Pharisees would not change. They thought they were righteous, that their ways were best, and they were not going to repent and turn to true worship. They preferred "the old wine" to the Spirit. Yet those who would change, who would long for "the new wine," would go out singing!

Review

Think about your walk with God: in your time alone with Him, in your church worship, in practicing His presence throughout the day. What warnings can you find personally from this week's study? What encouragement? What application?

_____

_____

_____

Prayer Time

In addition to any individual requests, pray for one another as you do next week's lesson, that God will give you understanding and breathe life into you. It is one of the most important lessons in this guide.

The Betrothing Bridegroom
Artist: Martin French (www.martinfrench.com)

Week 6
THE BETROTHING BRIDEGROOM

I will betroth you to Me forever.

—HOSEA 2:19

| MEMORY VERSE: |
| HOSEA 2:19–20 |

*E*ven in the portrait of *The Bridegroom*, we see tough and tender sides. There is a wonderful turn now in Hosea, where the strategy of the Lord changes from tough to tender, from the discipline that failed to the allurement of love. Many of the pictures and phrases remind us of an earthly bridegroom who woos his bride, who speaks gently to her, who delights her so much that she opens to him.

God uses pictures to turn the light on for us, and because we seem to grasp the beauty of earthly love, He uses that picture to help us understand what He longs for from us. Who wants a marriage that is about duty, drudgery, and dollars? When we look at our marriages like that, they become a tremendous burden, and we feel trapped. That's when we need to look back to the tender but magnetic power of courtship. Agur, in the book of Proverbs, used wonderful images to build to the best one of all:

> *There are three things that are too amazing for me,*
> *   four that I do not understand:*
> *the way of an eagle in the sky,*
> *   the way of a snake on a rock,*
> *the way of a ship on the high seas,*
> *   and the way of a man with a maiden.* (Proverbs 30:18–19 NIV)

Too often people equate Christianity with ethical behavior, with good works, with being good people; and while these *follow* the essence of Christianity, they are *not* the essence. Instead God intended both marriage and Christianity to be about love, about devotion, about playful companionship, like two eagles in the sky.

(Dee) My brother-in-law, John Frahm, has been a pastor, has taught at a Christian college, and heads up Alpha (a ministry God is using mightily in evangelism and revival) on North American

campuses. But though he was sound doctrinally, it wasn't until he became involved in Alpha that his understanding about Jesus truly went from his head to his heart. He told me recently,

> Falling in love with Jesus—that's really what it is all about. I was watching an Alpha video for about the third time when I suddenly found myself weeping. It was tremendous joy, and yet sorrow, at discovering this so late in life: that the Lord loves me so tenderly, and that this life is all about relationship with Him.
>
> I thought about my relationship with my wife, Sally, and how hurt I would be if she just came to me with a list of things she wanted me to do for her instead of expressing her affection and the desire to be with me. Everything is changing for me: my prayer time—I spend much more time in adoration, in song; my attitude—I'm understanding the concept of "practicing His presence."

How Jesus longs for a responsive bride, who sings Him love songs both when she is alone and when she is with the corporate bride; who is not just going through the motions but is truly loving Him. He longs to see her waiting, both in her individual quiet times and in church, in expectation, with her open Bible, for a "kiss"—the word that will move passionately into her heart. He wants us to unwrap His gifts with delight, gifts that flow in a steady stream from His hand every day: a crimson maple in the fall, the aroma of fresh coffee, the giggle of a child. He longs for us to talk to Him, to pray without ceasing, and to listen to Him, seeing Him everywhere, not forgetting that He is right at our sides, right within us! He wants to soar with us, so we will be like two eagles in the sky.

The Initiator in love, He takes the lead in this dance.

Day 5 in this study is a very important one, so if you are one who often doesn't finish her lesson, it would be better to skip days 2 and 3 than to miss days 4 and 5. Covenant is the essence of the bridegroom theme, and day 5 is possibly the most important day in this whole workbook.

VIDEO NOTES FOR WEEK 6

Don't cover these questions in discussion. Watch the video first, and then put your chairs in a circle to discuss this lesson.

1. It breaks His heart when we settle for R_____ and R_____ instead of R_____ and R_____.

2. One of the primary messages of both Hosea and John is that Christianity must penetrate the _____. If it does not, you may be one to whom the Lord says: I _____ _____ _____.

3. God permits believers tender names for Himself, like A_____ (dear Father) and I_____ (my Husband.)

4. God's people had tried and failed to obey the law, so now He looks forward to a day when He puts His S_____ in our hearts, and to another day, when we will be completely ch_____.

5. These mysterious words from Hosea were hidden for centuries but point to the key theme of covenant between God and His people:

> *And I will have mercy on her who had not obtained mercy;*
> *Then I will say to those who were not My people,*
> *"You _____ _____ _____!"*
> *And they shall say, "You _____ _____ _____!" (Hosea 2:23)*

WARM UP

Think of the playful companionship of two eagles gliding and circling each other in the sky. Then think about "the way of a man with a woman," the romance of catching her eye across the room, lifting her chin to kiss her, sending daffodils because he knows they are her favorite flowers.

What do you particularly remember from the video? Why?

What romantic picture pops into your head?

INTRODUCTION QUESTIONS

Please cover these vital questions in your discussion group.

1. Discuss Proverbs 30:18–19. What do these four pictures have in common, and why is the last the best?

   _____
   _____
   _____

2. What, according to this introduction, is the essence of Christianity? Do you think this is what most people think? Why it is vital to understand this?

   _____
   _____
   _____

Day 1

Softly and Tenderly

Today we will begin one of the most beautiful passages in Hosea. The Lord, the Bridegroom of Israel, had charged her "in court." He had allowed the thorns of her sin to pierce her. He had taken away her vineyards. He had exposed her in the eyes of her lovers. He had moved away from her for a time. Still, her heart was hard. She was not responding to Him.

Charles Spurgeon wrote:

> Other forms of power had been tried upon Israel. . . . He said to her, "I will hedge up thy way with thorns"; but she went right over the thorns. Then he said, "I will make a wall, that she shall not find her paths"; but she broke through the wall. . . . Though she found no mirth in sin, and the way of her transgressions was hard, yet Israel would not turn to God; but the sweet allurement of tenderness would succeed where all else had failed.[1]

Though she deserved to be abandoned, He did not forsake her. Softly and tenderly, He began to woo her. Where? Into the wilderness! There she would be alone with Him, away from her other lovers.

We can see an illustration of this in Israel's delivery from slavery in Egypt. At first she was a grateful bride, for when the Red Sea closed over her enemies, Miriam took up her timbrel and led all the women in song. But soon Israel forgot the Lord's great mercies. She murmured, she complained. He could see her hardening heart, but even though she betrayed Him, He did not give up. He led her into a long journey into the wilderness, where she was completely dependent on Him to sustain her. He fed her, He guided her, and He loved her. His purpose was to win her heart again.

Spurgeon put it like this:

> "I will allure her to myself," and then, "I will take her into the wilderness, she shall be in my company, and in nobody else's company." That is just what the grace of God does. She had forgotten him before, but now. . . . Instead of not thinking of him at all, he is in the first thoughts of the morning, and in the thoughts all day long.[2]

Read Hosea 2:14–23 as an overview.

1. Consider Hosea 2:14:

> *Therefore, behold, I will allure her . . .*

A. How is this a change in strategy from the first thirteen verses in Hosea 2?

_____

_____

Will bring her into the wilderness.

B. Why is it that being alone with someone that you love can help you to fall in love all over again?

_____

_____

C. Have circumstances, rather than choices, ever caused you to be alone with the Lord—such as a move away from friends and family, a time of illness, or the loss of someone you tended to run to more than the Lord? Share something about it and how it impacted your relationship with the Lord.

_____

_____

In Hosea's day, Israel's sin was religious syncretism. It was a form of idolatry, worshiping other gods in addition to the only true God. We do this today both corporately and individually.

Perhaps you are thinking, *I don't worship other gods.* Perhaps your doctrine *is* sound, and you are immersed enough in the Word and good expositional preaching that the philosophies of other religions are not leading you astray. However, we need to look clearly at our lives to see where our trust is. Often, it is in ourselves, making us unduly concerned with our own reputations. It may be in our wealth or in various comforts we place in our lives. God may have to take them away to show us what unreliable gods these are. But most often, as women we are prone to trust in people, to cling to them too tightly, and to idolize them, much as the Israelites idolized Baal. Often it is to these people we run instead of to God.

And speak comfort to her . . .

D. This exact phrase actually describes a man speaking tenderly to a woman. It is an idiom that means "to woo, to speak to the heart." Ruth used this idiom to describe Boaz's manner with her in Ruth 2:13. Find the ways he spoke comfort to her heart in Ruth 2:11–12.

_____

_____

E. This phrase is also used in a passage from Isaiah made famous by Handel's *Messiah.* What did the Lord say in Isaiah 40:1–2?

_____

_____

2. Tomorrow we will look deeply at Hosea 2:15, which makes a comparison to how God dealt with His bride in the Exodus. In preparation, read Psalm 126.

A. How did the psalmist describe those the Lord delivered from slavery in verses 1–2?

_____

_____

B. Can you think of a time when the Lord astounded you with His mercy? A time when He opened the prison door and you felt almost as if it were a dream? If so, share something about it.

_____

_____

C. God's people *had* suffered great hardship, and there had been weeping. But then, God changed His strategy and "allured" His bride. What pictures did the psalmist use to describe the transformation in verses 5–6?

_____

_____

D. Often fruitfulness follows a time of deliverance from captivity. How is this true in this psalm? Have you experienced this in your own life? If so, share briefly.

_____

_____

3. So often when we go through a time of great trouble or trial, we are hurting so much that we are numb. But later we are able to hear the Lord's tender voice, His comfort. Often this occurs through Scripture, but He may speak to us in other ways. If the Lord has spoken tenderly to you in a time of trouble, helping you to "go out singing," share briefly what happened.

_____

_____

_____

Day 2

Wonderful Merciful Savior

"Be still, and know that [I AM] God," He said in Psalm 46:10. Be still. Then praise Him with worship and your whole heart, soul, and mind.

Begin learning your memory passage.

R. C. Sproul said, "Even in judgment, even in the 'bill of divorce,' even in the exile, even in the defeat: [Each is intended] to be *corrective* wrath designed to bring His people back, to lead them to repentance that the covenant may be renewed."[3] God allured Israel into the wilderness. Why? That He may have her full attention!

How many of us, particularly as women, cling too tightly to people? This is why He sometimes has to allure us into the wilderness, away from all the people and the things we tend to depend on. There are going to be times in each of our lives when we realize the only One who can truly help us is God. Author Beth Moore has said that Jesus had a large circle of friends (the twelve disciples), an intimate circle (Peter, James, John), and finally, there were times, as in Gethsemane, when He had only His Father. How beautifully this was illustrated in the movie *The Passion of the Christ*.

Sometimes only God will be there for us. If we don't understand this, God may have to show us by taking us alone into the wilderness. It is only then that we can discover a whole different devotion toward the only One who will never fail us.

It is in the wilderness where we may finally be able to hear his voice. C. S. Lewis says God whispers in our pleasure but shouts in our pain. "The Valley of Achor" certainly illustrated a time of pain for the Israelites. This was a desolate plain where the Israelites stoned Achan, one of their own, because of his sin. This historical incident, recorded in Joshua 7, was a model of what was about to happen to Israel. Hosea could see that Israel was going to experience the judgment of God and be taken captive by the Assyrians (Hosea 11:5). But that door of judgment would also be a door of hope leading to purification and restoration with God. This is a pattern with God: His discipline does not last forever. Weeping may endure for the night, but joy comes in the morning.

Hosea 2:15 is a critical verse, so we will look at each phrase carefully.

1. *I will give her her vineyards from there.*
    A. Find the contrast between this verse and Hosea 2:12.

    _____

    _____

    B. When the backslider or prodigal returns to Christ, often the very things that he lost are restored to him, pressed down and flowing over. How was that true in the story of the prodigal son (Luke 15:20–22)?

    _____

    _____

    C. Can you remember a time when God dealt with you, you repented, and then you truly had your vineyards "restored"? Perhaps it was the joy of His presence, perhaps it was a relationship restored. If so, share something about it.

    _____

    _____

2. *And the Valley of Achor as a door of hope.*

A. At times in Scripture, God's judgment seems severe, but it simply should remind us of His holiness. Read Joshua 6:15–17 and state the context of the story.

_____

_____

B. What did Joshua specifically tell the people *not* to do? Why (Joshua 6:18–19)?

_____

_____

The accursed things were the gold and silver, including the gold and silver gods. All plunder belonged to the Lord in this first battle.

C. What did Achan do? What was the result (Joshua 7:1)?

_____

_____

D. When Joshua confronted Achan, what did he confess? How was he disciplined? What then happened to the anger of the Lord (Joshua 7:19–26)?

_____

_____

Whenever a believer experiences death because of the judgment of God, it seems severe. The judgment of Uzzah (2 Samuel 6), and the judgment of Ananias and Sapphira (Acts 5), purified the body of believers, reminding them that they were dealing with a holy God. It is helpful to remember that the believers who died in judgment, did, if they knew the Lord, go to be with Him in paradise.

E. This valley became known as the Valley of Achor, a symbol of the judgment of God. Hosea could see ahead, and he knew that God's people were going to pass through a similar door. What was it, according to Hosea 11:5–7?

_____

_____

F. Yet just as the people in Joshua's day experienced the presence and power of God, so Hosea could see that the "valley of trouble" would become a "door of hope." If one is experiencing the judgment of God in her life right now, what lessons can she learn?

_____

_____

Kathy often tells women: "Don't despise the circumstance you are in. It may be the very thing He is using to draw you to Him."

3. *She shall sing there, as in the days of her youth, as in the day when she came up from the land of Egypt.*

   A. Describe God's bride when God first delivered her from Egypt (Exodus 15:1–5; 20–21).

   _____

   _____

   B. Describe yourself when you first came to know Jesus and experienced His forgiveness.

   _____

   _____

   C. Describe an area of new deliverance in your life.

   _____

   _____

   D. What promise does this passage hold for you personally?

   _____

   _____

The gospel of John is the fulfillment of many of the promises in Hosea and the prophets. The Law was holy, but God's bride had not been able to keep the old covenant. She needed to have her heart of stone replaced with a heart of flesh; she needed the Holy Spirit; she needed "rivers of living water" flowing within her so that she could be a responsive bride. Earlier in this study we touched on the story of the Samaritan woman, and here we will look at it more closely, for it beautifully pictures our key verse.

This encounter is surprising, for Jesus crossed both the barriers of race and gender. "The Mishnah [the entire body of Jewish law] indicates that Samaritan women were regarded as perpetually unclean. *Niddah* 4:1 [the Jewish laws of separation] indicates that these women are menstruants from the cradle."[4] But there was Jesus, waiting for her, asking to drink from her jar, her "unclean" vessel. No wonder the disciples were shocked. It is such a beautiful picture of the new era opened to a people "who were not My people" (Hosea 2:23). It is also a picture of hope of faithfulness for His bride because of the living water, representing the Spirit He will give.

4. Read the whole story in John 4:1–42.

   A. Many Jews despised the Samaritans and avoided Samaria. But Jesus did not follow that practice. The Samaritan woman, because of her reputation, waited until the hottest time of the day so that she would be alone at the well. But when she arrived, she found Jesus. Describe her encounter with Jesus and how He "spoke tenderly to her."

   _____

   _____

   B. What did Jesus know about her background (John 4:16–18)?

   _____

   _____

C. In what ways was the woman in a "wilderness"? In what ways do you think Jesus's words were both painful and yet comforting to her?

_____

_____

D. What question did the woman ask? Explain how Jesus's answer showed it was time for a new era (John 4:19–25).

_____

_____

The reply hints at the time Hosea promised. "The Messiah is the giver of the Spirit . . . creating worshipers of the Father who worship in spirit and truth. . . . This leads naturally into the question about the great figure of the promised new era, the Messiah."[5]

E. What did Jesus tell the woman about His identity (John 4:26)?

_____

_____

F. What evidence do you find that the woman responded positively to Jesus? How did she "go out singing"?

_____

_____

Day 3

Change My Heart, O God

Sing to Him, and memorize the week's passage.

(Kathy) My closest friends were so gracious to throw me a housewarming party when I moved to Nashville. I was humbled at the idea of it; single women don't have the sweet experience of friends throwing showers for them. To think I could go to some of my favorite stores, check off a list of all the things I loved in those stores, and have my friends go and buy them for me. Was it really going to happen?

Off I went to register at some of those stores, looking at kitchen, bed, and bath things galore. I was standing in Williams-Sonoma, checking out the array of kitchen utensils I knew I would never use—I boil a mean pot of water—but I knew other people would need them if they cooked at my house. While looking at the knives, I suddenly felt overwhelmed. _What do I know about carving, paring, and filleting? I just need something that cuts well._ So I asked a store clerk for some help. I told her I was registering, so she took out my form to help me mark some items. The first thing she said was, "Well, most brides . . ."

A pain hit my heart I don't usually feel. As most of you know, I've often described my contentment in my singleness. For some reason, that day her words pierced me far more than the knives I was looking at could have.

Wow. I have never, and might not ever, experience being a bride.

My friend Glenna was with me, and she tapped me on the shoulder as my eyes welled up with tears. She's a little bit older than me and has been part of my prayer team, so she knows some of my deepest heart. She whispered, *"You are a bride."*

How ironic that I've written and spoken to thousands of women about this, boldly proclaiming my betrothment. Because I was taken off guard, it was such a tender moment to be gently reminded that I was His. An unspoken joy came back in my heart that helped me finish my registering, knowing that my Bridegroom was with me.

He loves me with an everlasting love. Isaiah said,

> *And as the bridegroom rejoices over the bride,*
> *So shall your God rejoice over you.* (Isaiah 62:5)

Zephaniah said,

> *The Mighty One, will save;*
> *He will rejoice over you with gladness,*
> *He will quiet you with His love,*
> *He will rejoice over you with singing.* (Zephaniah 3:17)

Hosea says,

> *I will betroth you to Me forever.* (Hosea 2:19)

Jesus *has* been a tender Bridegroom to me, but this isn't just for single women. *Everyone* who has come under the shadow of His wings, who has trusted in so great a salvation—marrieds, singles, Jews, Gentiles, men, women, and children—we are all the bride of Christ. When Paul was speaking of how husbands should cherish their wives and how wives should respond to those husbands with respect, suddenly he made a shift from the earthly love relationship to the spiritual one and said,

> *This is a great mystery, but I speak concerning Christ and the church.* (Ephesians 5:32)

What was he saying? He was saying that each of us who believes is part of the bride of Christ. It breaks His heart when we settle for ritual and religion instead of romance and relationship. God is looking for a love relationship with us.

Hosea looked forward to a day when all believers would embrace God as such. He said,

> *"And it shall be, in that day,"*
> *Says the LORD,*

"That you will call Me 'My Husband,'
And no longer call Me 'My Master.'" (Hosea 2:16)

It isn't wrong to see God as our Master and Lord—He is, though He longs to be more than that. He longs to be the Lover of our souls. What is actually happening here is that the Hebrew word for "master" *(ba'li)* sounds a lot like *Baal,* the false god the Israelites had worshiped. Sometimes a good word can become perverted. For example, *tyrant* used to simply mean "king," but there were so many bad kings that *tyrant* came to mean an evil king. Therefore, it would truly be an insult to call a king a tyrant, because the name became negative.

In the same way, because the Israelites had worshiped Baal, calling the true God a name that sounded like Baal was very hurtful to Him. It would be like an adulterous wife whose husband has forgiven her, whispering the name of her past lover in their marriage bed.

Read Hosea 2:16.

1. One day, what would Israelites call the Lord? What would they not call Him?

   _____

   _____

   _____

2. The word *master* in Hebrew sounded a lot like *Baal.* Why would this be an abomination to the Lord?

   _____

   _____

   _____

3. The Israelites had taken the good gifts God had given them and offered them to Baal (Hosea 2:8). Also, Baal worship involved temple prostitutes and other abominations. How did Jeremiah describe the behavior of the Israelites in Jeremiah 2:20?

   _____

   _____

   _____

God longs for so much in His relationship with us. Though He *is* our Master, He yearns for us to serve Him out of love rather than fear. Of course He longs for intense affection and devotion rather than fear and trembling that might be associated with being enslaved.

4. Our relationship with the Lord changes as it matures.
   A. What change did Jesus promise believing Jews in John 8:31–32?

   _____

   _____

B. What change did Jesus describe in His relationship with His disciples in John 15:14–15?

_____

_____

C. How did John describe love perfected in 1 John 4:17–19?

_____

_____

As our confidence in the Lord's love grows, we are less afraid of people, of abandoning ourselves to Him, and of the difficulties of life in general. We also do not need to be afraid of God's judgment, for He has promised us mercy.

D. Give an example from your life of how His love has "cast out fear," giving you confidence to move ahead in faith.

_____

_____

Believers are permitted special names for the Lord. One is *Abba,* which is, literally, "Dear Father."[6] Another is *ishi,* which is a tender name for a husband, in contrast to *ba'li* (lord), which is also a name wives used out of respect for their husbands (1 Peter 3:6). However, in this case, *ba'li* sounded too much like Baal, and the Lord permitted the Israelites to use the tender and endearing name of *Ishi.*

Remembering the Lord's steadfast and tender love for you, no matter how you fail Him, is vital. Too many believers think they must be good in order to keep the Lord loving them, when His love is steadfast. But when you truly realize His love is here to stay, it can give you the courage to live a life of confidence.

5. What would the Lord do to help Israel be pure, according to Hosea 2:17?

_____

_____

_____

Though we realize it is only by His grace we are saved, too many of us try to live the Christian life in our own effort. Bryan Chapell, Covenant Seminary president, wrote,

> But now with the living presence of the God of Creation in us, though we are still in the same bodies, we are fundamentally different creatures (1 Peter 1:23). . . . Our new nature enables us increasingly to discern and defeat the forces of evil in our lives. As our sanctification progresses there is an ever-widening swatch of the Spirit's influence in our lives.[7]

Each time you, through the Spirit, defeat a "Baal" (a temptation, a false support) in your life, Christ's power grows stronger in you.

6. What are the names of the Baals in your life? When you allow the Spirit living in you to defeat them, how does the power in you increase?

_____

_____

_____

One day, and what a day that will be, the struggle will be over, and our natures will be completely changed. Charles Spurgeon wrote,

> Oh! what a blessed thought: the name of Baalim out of my mouth, sin out of my heart, the lustful glance from my eye, evil things from my imagination, all gone! Oh! will we not praise our Lord in the bright moment when we wake up in his likeness, when our glorified spirit shall be white as driven snow, in the glad companionship of the immaculate, the pure, the perfect? Oh, what joyous shouts we shall raise then! What choral symphonies, what bursts of song, what hallelujahs of gratitude! [8]

7. Describe the peace of the new covenant in the future kingdom, according to Hosea 2:18. How will God completely transform humanity and the animal kingdom?

_____

_____

_____

Day 4

Love Found a Way

Pray through the memory passage:

> I will betroth you to Me forever;
> Yes, I will betroth you to Me
> In righteousness and justice,
> In lovingkindness and mercy;
> I will betroth you to Me in faithfulness,
> And you shall know the LORD. (Hosea 2:19–20)

Pray this prayer to prepare you for day 4:

Lord, thank You for betrothing Yourself to me.
Thank You for Your faithfulness in this relationship,
I can possess everything You are.
Continue Your work in me, giving me Your heart of righteousness and justice,
Your lovingkindness, mercy, and faithfulness.

God's bride had been unable to keep the law. Though the law was holy and good, she could not live up to it. So the Lord promised a new covenant, when He would write His law on her heart, when He would put His Spirit within her, when He would betroth to her the qualities she so desperately needed to be a pure and holy bride. The scene in the "divorce" court was over. He had courted her again, alluring her, winning her heart. Next He was going to betroth her to Himself again.

Betrothal, in biblical days, was as binding as marriage. Though the marriage had not been consummated, a betrothed woman was considered a wife. J. B. Phillips version paraphrases this passage as follows:

> *I will take you to be my wife for ever.*
> *I will take you to be my wife rightly and justly,*
> *I will take you in kindness and mercy.*
> *I will take you to be my wife in faithfulness,*
> *And you shall know the Lord.* (Hosea 2:19–20 PHILLIPS)

1. What light does each of the following passages shed on the seriousness of betrothal?
   A. Deuteronomy 22:23–24

   _____

   _____

   B. Matthew 1:18–19

   _____

   _____

2. Read Hosea 2:19–20.
   A. What phrase did the Lord keep repeating?

   _____

   _____

   B. What significance do you see in the repetition?

   _____

   _____

Coming three times in quick succession, the word *betroth* gives a note of eagerness and warmth to what is promised. It makes a new beginning, with all the freshness of first love, rather than the weary patching up of difference—and this is appropriate, since a new covenant brings with it new life.[9]

C. What five characteristics did the Lord promise to give to His bride?

_____

_____

In biblical days, a bridegroom gave a bride price, a "down payment." Here, the spiritual parallel is that the qualities the Lord listed are a sort of bride price. He would protect, love, and do all these things for her, for that was His character; but—and this is the exciting part—He was also going to implant, to sow in her heart, those qualities that would enable her to keep her part of the covenant!

D. Jeremiah also looked forward to that day when a different spirit would be in the bride. Describe it, according to Jeremiah 31:33.

_____

_____

E. How did Ezekiel describe the new heart of the bride in Ezekiel 11:19–20?

_____

_____

F. What was the first quality the Lord would give His bride? Find its fulfillment in Romans 5:17. What do you think this means?

_____

_____

G. What was the next quality that would be in His bride? How do you see the Lord longing for this in His bride in Amos 5:21–24?

_____

_____

H. What was the third quality? This is a famous Hebrew word, *hesed,* which is the essence of the character of God and can be seen in Lamentations 3:22–23. Describe it.

_____

_____

I. The quality of unfailing love is the quality that had been so lacking in His bride. It is the quality we so desperately need, for we are unfaithful to God and to one another. What does Proverbs 20:6 tell us?

_____

_____

J. How eager the Lord was to cancel the name Lo-Ruhamah (No Mercy)! What was the next quality He would give? And what is the final quality Hosea mentioned?

_____

_____

K. What will be the final result of this changed heart, according to Hosea 2:20?

_____

_____

Those of you who did the *Living in Love with Jesus* Bible study may remember that the promises in 1 John say that we become like the One who gave us spiritual birth. It is a process, but as we walk in the light, more of His light shines in us; as we love our brother, more of His love grows in us; and as we live by the truth, more of His truth strengthens us. One day, it will be complete, and we will be like Him when we see Him as He is (1 John 3:2).

Day 5
From This Moment On

Continue praying Scripture:

> *And I will have mercy on her who had not obtained mercy;*
> *Then I will say to those who were not My people,*
> *"You are My people!"*
> *And they shall say, "You are my God!"* (Hosea 2:23)

This prayer will help prepare you for day 5:

> Thank You, Lord, for giving me mercy, for taking me as Your bride.
> I renew my "marriage vows" to You of faithfulness, honor, and love—
> I take You as my Husband. You are my God!

Review your memory passage.

The betrothal scene continues at the close of Hosea 2, moving into an actual wedding, where the Lord took Israel as His bride, and she took Him as her Husband. The land that He had once judged and made barren was planted and made fruitful. It's a beautiful and central picture, and one that is being fulfilled right now under the promise of the new covenant.

1. Read Hosea 2:21–23.
   A. The land of Israel is personified here as having a dialogue with the Lord. Israel had cried out to Him, and He would respond. How can you see dialogue in this poetic passage?

   _____

   _____

B. Describe the eagerness of the Lord and the change in the barren land of Jezreel (vv. 21–22).

_____

_____

C. In verse 23, what change does God foresee for "No Mercy" and "Not My People"?

_____

_____

D. This has been fulfilled, at least in part. Describe the fulfillment in 1 Peter 2:9–10. What does this mean to you personally?

_____

_____

2. The closing verse in Hosea 2 is key to the whole message of the Bible. It puts us in awe of a sovereign God to see how this is woven throughout time.
   A. Long before Hosea, what did Moses prophesy in Deuteronomy 32:19–21?

_____

_____

B. What do you see in Romans 9:22–26?

_____

_____

C. Because of the infidelity of the Jews, we as Gentiles became God's bride. What hope, however, do you see for the Jews in Romans 10:19?

_____

_____

3. One of the keys to understanding what is important to God is His use of repetition. Look at each of the following repeated thoughts and see if you can glean anything new from them. (There are additional passages with these same words that we'll not study due to time constraints.)
   A. Ezekiel 37:26–27

_____

_____

B. 2 Corinthians 6:16

_____

_____

C. 1 Peter 2:9–10

_____

_____

The heart of the Bridegroom is that we are in covenant with the living God, who desires oneness, intimacy, and faithfulness. How can we carry this out? By living every day in a way that expresses, "You are my God!"

(*Dee*) My pastor, Mike Lano, explains that the primary purpose of Sunday worship is not evangelism, teaching, or even praise—though those elements should be parts of the service. The purpose of Sunday worship should be a renewal of our covenant with God. Every week, because of our bent toward sin, of our tendency to be unfaithful brides, we need to come to Him in confession. We will find Him eager to renew the covenant.

Consider seeing your worship service as a dialogue to renew your covenant. Let me show you what I mean through our typical order of worship.

Order of Worship	*Explanation*	*Dialogue*
Call to worship	Music played	You are my people!
Confession of sin	Scriptural prayer by people	You are my God!
Promise of forgiveness	Scriptural promise read by elder	You are my people!
Hymns and choruses	Expressing thanks and needs	You are my God!
The Scripture passage read	Word from God	You are my people!
Offering	Expressing love	You are my God!
The Word is expounded	Word from God	You are my people!
Hymn of response	"Bear fruit, O Word from Heaven"	You are my God!
Benediction	His promise to be with us	You are my people!

4. Your order of worship may be slightly different, but think about it, and see if you can see a similar dialogue.

A. How does God initiate the dialogue in your worship service?

_____

_____

B. What is your initial response (confession, praise . . .)?

_____

_____

C. Do you have the sense that God speaks to you through His servant, your pastor?

_____

_____

D. How will your attitude through the worship service affect your response? Do you see yourself as a spectator, performer, or someone engaging in a dialogue? Explain.

_____

_____

5. What is the mystery revealed, according to Colossians 1:27?

_____

_____

_____

It is vital to see that this closing verse in Hosea 2 is the mystery that is revealed in the New Testament. As R. C. Sproul says, this "passage went unnoticed by the vast majority of people for centuries and centuries and centuries. . . . The prophetic utterance here was veiled and cloaked in mystery." He continues,

> Do you realize that those of you who are Gentiles have no original intrinsic claim to the Kingdom of God? Salvation is to the Jews. Israel is the chosen nation. We had no inheritance. . . . You were nothing. No people. And God has said to you, "Ammi [my people]." That is the mystery of mysteries. Through the irony of the very sin of Israel, that where their wickedness abounded, God's grace abounded. Through their prostitution, you were invited to the wedding. . . . Hardness in part has happened to Israel that the time of the Gentiles should happen. And I for one see hope in this passage for an even greater restoration for the original children of the covenant.[10]

Review

What are some of the central truths John and Hosea communicated when they pictured Jesus as our Bridegroom or our Husband?

Prayer Time

Break into groups of four or five and choose a worship facilitator.

Worship Facilitator:

Hear the Word of the Lord:
> _"I will betroth you to Me forever;_
> _Yes, I will betroth you to Me."_

Group Responds:

And we say to You, O Lord, "We take you as our God!"

Worship Facilitator:

Hear the Word of the Lord:
I will have mercy on her who had not obtained mercy.
Then I will say to those who were not My people,
"You are My people!"

Group Responds:

And we say to You, O God, "You are my God!"

Close by singing "Step by Step."

STEP BY STEP

> O God, You are my God, and I will ever praise
>   You.
> O God, You are my God, and I will ever praise
>   You.
> I will seek You in the morning,
> And I will learn to walk in Your ways.
> And step by step You'll lead me,
> And I will follow You all of my days.

The Redeemer
Artist: Martin French (www.martinfrench.com)

Week 7
THE REDEEMER

There are many who struggle to survive in life, many who have been used and abused in the name of love, many who have been sacrificed on the altars of pleasure and "freedom." But the freedom the world offers is, in reality, false. Too many have awakened one day to discover they are in bondage, and they have no idea how to escape it. It is for people such as these that I wrote Redeeming Love.

—FRANCINE RIVERS

| MEMORY VERSE: |
| HOSEA 2:23 |

*K*athy) One of my favorite books is Francine Rivers's *Redeeming Love,* a historical fiction account of Hosea. Sometimes as I'm working in my office, I'll glance at my bookshelf, and just seeing the binding of this treasure, I am warmed and comforted. I am sweetly reminded of the unfailing love that her main character, Michael Hosea, possessed for his unfaithful bride, Angel. I probably could still find some tear stains on the pages; I identified with Angel, for I was so amazed and broken by Hosea's powerful devotion.

> She hurt.
> He loved.
> She retreated.
> He loved.
> She betrayed.
> He loved.
> He loved and then he loved some more.

I was feeling sad when I came to the end of the book, because I fell more deeply in love with Michael with each chapter. When I went to bed that night, I had a strange, lonely feeling. I kept asking myself, *What is wrong with you?* I realized I had been comforted in the last couple of days by the presence of Michael—and I missed him. And then I realized, *I have Him . . . Jesus.* How easily I forget. I closed my eyes, knowing that I was loved not by a fictional hero, but by a forever Bridegroom.

(*Dee*) I found it intriguing that Francine Rivers especially had in mind those who have had a hard start in life, "who have been used and abused in the name of love." I have watched in awe as Jesus has acted as Redeemer to our daughter Beth—not only in salvation, but also in rescuing her from a fallen world and her own bondage to sin.

Abused as a baby, she lost an arm. Then she was abandoned. Someone found her and took her to the hospital. She then spent the first twelve years of her life in an orphanage where she experienced more abuse. Not only did some emotionally sick adults care for her, but the children, who were all handicapped in some way, developed a lifestyle of picking on each other—much the way you see happening in a prison, where hurt people hurt people. Yet God heard her cry.

I have often told of how my husband and I prayed about the decision to adopt and how, during prayer, my husband clearly heard "a little girl who was crying." That little girl was Beth, and we flew to her orphanage in Thailand to bring her back as our daughter. Though she knew no English, we put her in school, where she not only learned English but earned a full-tuition scholarship to college. Her English is still a bit broken, as Thai and English are so different. Beth is still painfully shy, so on the video, Beth and I agreed I would tell her story. Imagine her surprise when Kathy called her up onstage! It's a tender moment.

As Beth's mother, I am astounded at the number of wonderful godly people God has provided for her: friends, mentors, and counselors. I have a dear friend who offered to have Beth come to her house daily to learn English. Jan tutored Beth for three years, pouring love and life into her. The Lord provided some unusually mature teenage girls to love Beth in her high school years. Right now a devout young woman is mentoring Beth, going through Dan Allender's *The Wounded Heart* with her, helping her resolve deep hurts from the past.

Beth graduates this year and wants to move to a bigger city to pursue a career. Recently my daughter-in-law said, "Please have her move to Kansas City and live with us. John can build her a little apartment downstairs and she can live with us as long as she wants!" I have often said to Beth, "Do you see it, honey? Wherever you turn, God is sending someone to help you! He surely loves you." She nods, her dark eyes shining.

Recently Beth received an assignment at the University of Nebraska to bring a song or poem and give a short speech on why it was meaningful to her. She brought a medley of songs sung by Point of Grace, all focused on the grace of God. She alternated between her story, told in broken English, and the medley from her tape recorder. I know she stunned the class. They weren't expecting this painfully shy beauty to share so openly and honestly. She certainly didn't lead into her story gently, for she began, "I lost my arm when I a baby. But I not die. Somebody found me." Then Beth pushed Play on the tape recorder and the class heard,

> Who am I that You would love me so gently?
> Who am I that You would recognize my name?
> Lord, who am I that You would speak to me so softly?
> Conversation with the Lord most high, who am I?

She continued, "In the orphanage in Thailand, I have no place to belong. People hurt me and I, myself, hurt people. But somebody care and brought me to America. Now I belong in a family."

> Amazing grace, how sweet the sound that saved a wretch like me,
> I once was lost but now I'm found,
> Was blind but now I see.

And the more I sing that sweet old song,

The more I understand that I do not comprehend

This love that's coming from your hand.

Then Beth went on: "It still taking me awhile to realize that someone love me enough to draw me out of my darkness. Not knowing what the futures may have in store for me. But I am glad to find someone who loves me as I am."

Who am I that You would love me so gently?

Who am I that You would recognize my name?

Lord, who am I that You would speak to me so softly?

Conversation with the Lord most high, who am I?

As she concluded her talk, people were visibly weeping, as she said, "I struggle with hurts in my heart. I struggle with bad habits. But God care. God sending people who care about me just as I am, care about my hurts, care about helping me find another life."

Grace, grace, God's grace,

Grace that will pardon and cleanse within,

Grace, grace, God's great grace,

Grace that is greater than all my sin.

We have a Redeemer who longs to rescue us from our chains. No matter our darkness, His light is brighter. No matter the price for our chains, He will pay it. No matter how deep our pit, His arm is longer. No matter where we go, He will be there.

VIDEO NOTES FOR WEEK 7

Don't cover these statements in discussion. Watch the video first, and then put your chairs in a circle to discuss this lesson.

1. The word *redeemer* comes from the Hebrew word _____and reminded people of wonderful things like_____ and_____.

2. The first time this portrait occurs is in the book of _____.

3. The name Hosea is derived, like Joshua and Jesus, from the Hebrew word meaning _____ or _____.

4. In Hosea, the bride is redeemed through a few coins and bushels of barley, but in John, "the bride" is redeemed through the _____.

WARM UP

What is one of your favorite romantic books, fairy tales, or movies in which a hero, a "Prince Charming" or a godly man, rescues someone in distress?

What do you particularly remember from the video? Why?

INTRODUCTION QUESTION

Please cover this question in your discussion group.

1. Look at the artist's portrait *The Redeemer* preceding this chapter. In a sentence, describe the various feelings Gomer might have had. Can you identify with this in any way? If so, how?

_____

_____

_____

Day 1

I Know That My Redeemer Lives

Frideric Handel said that he was lifted into an ecstatic vision when he wrote his *Messiah*. One of the most stirring pieces in the *Messiah* is "I Know That My Redeemer Liveth." Job uttered these words in the midst of intense suffering, when his skin was oozing with open sores. Still he was faithful, longing to leave a legacy honoring God. In answer to his prayer, Job is

> momentarily lifted out of his despair and rocketed into a kind of prophetic ecstasy where he "utters mysteries with his spirit" (1 Cor. 14:2). The entire book rises to an amazing climax here, a climax centering on this mysterious, thrilling word "Redeemer."[1]

How amazing that the first portrait of Christ as Redeemer occurred here in this ancient book. It is where Job had a vision of the return of Christ: that magnificent day when the dead in Christ will rise, and in exchange for their decayed flesh and decomposed bodies they will receive strong, healthy bodies. Job absolutely knew that one day he would see his Redeemer face to face, standing upon the earth.

For I know that my Redeemer lives,
And He shall stand at last on the earth;
And after my skin is destroyed, this I know,
That in my flesh I shall see God,
Whom I shall see for myself,
And my eyes shall behold, and not another.
How my heart yearns within me. (Job 19:25–27)

The actual Hebrew word for "redeemer" is *go'el*. Mike Mason continues, describing what this word meant to Jewish ears:

> It was a delicious word, a passionate word, a word that smacked of chains falling off, of finding buried treasure, of suddenly having more good fortune fall into one's lap than one had ever dreamed or imagined.[2]

Mason comments that the word *go'el* "happens to come remarkably close to another word that can ignite our hearts: gospel."[3]

1. What is the Hebrew word for "redeemer"? How does author Mike Mason describe the impact that word had on Jewish hearts?

   _____

   _____

   _____

2. Give a brief summary of each of the following passages:
   A. Job 1:8–12

   _____

   _____

   B. Job 1:13–22

   _____

   _____

   C. Job 2:1–10

   _____

   _____

Job's misery continued to multiply not only physically but emotionally as his friends offered him rebuke rather than consolation.

3. Each of his friends spoke a truth from God but misapplied it to Job, for God had already affirmed Job's blamelessness in His sight (Job 1:1, 8).

A. What truth did Eliphaz misapply to Job in Job 4:8–9?

_____

_____

B. What truth did he misapply to Job in Job 5:17?

_____

_____

C. How did Zophar increase Job's pain with another misapplication in Job 11:6?

_____

_____

4. Describe Job's longing according to Job 19:23–24.

_____

_____

5. God answered Job's prayer with a vision, and Job prophesied.
    A. Of what truths was Job confident, according to Job 19:25?

_____

_____

"For I know," what a splendid burst of confidence this is, right out of the depth of his sorrow, like some wondrous star that suddenly blazes upon the brow of the blackest night, or like the sudden rising of the morning sun![4]

B. Do you *know* your Redeemer lives? How, according to 1 John 5:12–13, can you have the confidence Job had?

_____

_____

C. Do you think that Jesus's standing on the earth referred to His first or second coming? Why?

_____

_____

Charles Spurgeon believes it is both. Since Job will see Him in His "flesh," it must include the Second Coming, when the dead in Christ will rise (1 Thessalonians 4:16; 1 Corinthians 15:52). Mike Mason says,

> The Bible plainly teaches that resurrection is not a phenomenon that will tran-
> spire up in Heaven but rather—much more shockingly—right here on earth.
> Here is where death occurs; here is where the dead will rise. To dust our bod-
> ies were consigned, from dust they shall be reclaimed. Listen: the very graves

will open their mouths, and the dead will spring out of them and begin walking around—just as Jesus did on Easter morning![5]

D. What "exchange" is the Redeemer going to accomplish, according to Job 19:26?

_____

_____

E. What does this mean to you personally? A person who is blind wants to see in glory, a person who has struggled with a certain addiction or disease longs to know complete healing. What will it be for you?

_____

_____

F. Describe the confidence and emotion of Job 19:27.

_____

_____

Mason asks, "Where did Job get this word [for *redeemer*] and what did it mean to him?"

> In Hebrew the word is *go'el,* and it had two general applications. In daily usage its primary meaning was "one who restores," or "one who puts something back into its original or pristine condition." For Christians who know the Lord not only as their Creator but as their re-Creator, this primary meaning of the word *go'el* is rich in connotation.[6]

In this sense, the Redeemer has similarities to the Word, for He re-creates us with His mighty power, wisdom, and love.

The other application of *go'el* is best illustrated by the stories of Ruth and Gomer: two women in destitute circumstances who were redeemed by a "Prince Charming," a man who was related to them, who cared about them, and who was willing to pay a price to rescue them. We will begin these wonderful pictures tomorrow.

Day 2
There Is a Redeemer

Spend some time praising the Lord for the various chains He has redeemed you from.
Reflect on Psalm 107:10–16:

> *Some sat in darkness and the deepest gloom,*
> *prisoners suffering in iron chains,*

for they had rebelled against the words of God
   and despised the counsel of the Most High.
So he subjected them to bitter labor;
   they stumbled, and there was no one to help.
Then they cried to the LORD in their trouble,
   and he saved them from their distress.
He brought them out of darkness and the deepest gloom
   and broke away their chains.
Let them give thanks to the LORD for his unfailing love
   and his wonderful deeds for men,
for he breaks down gates of bronze
   and cuts through bars of iron. (Psalm 107:10–16 NIV)

Begin your memory work.

In *Falling in Love with Jesus*, we looked carefully at the book of Ruth and at Boaz, the "kinsman-redeemer" who was a picture of Jesus. Ruth was destitute: a widow, a foreigner, a woman without land, without family . . . and along came Boaz. He rescued her from her poverty and trouble.

Dee tells the contemporary parallel story of her friend Jill, a modern-day Ruth who met a modern-day Boaz. Jill lost her husband in a farming accident and then eventually was unable to keep up the farm and had to move to town. But a few years later a wonderful man named Keith married Jill. Keith (our Boaz) made it possible for Jill and the children to move back to the farm they had known and loved. He filled Jill's longing for a loving husband and godly father for her four young children.

(*Kathy*) I've had the pleasure of getting to know Jill because she now works as Dee's manager. I had heard Dee talk about her in our presentations and was always moved by her story. Jill is a "salt of the earth" kind of gal. She is lovely and would do anything for anyone. Lots of times when I call the Brestin home, Jill answers.

One of those times she invited me to come over for dinner at the farm. I told her that I would be delighted. She then went on to tell me that Keith would love to take me out to the fields to show me what he does. I just smiled because I'd finally get to meet Boaz.

The day came, and Jill told Dee that she'd go before us and meet us out in the cornfields where Keith was working. We drove down lots of dirt roads and finally stopped at an endless row of cornstalks. I thought, *We're not fooling around here. This is the real deal.* Before I knew it, I saw this gigantic green machine coming our way. I thought, *What on earth . . . ?* I was told it was a combine. When it came to a stop, I saw this handsome man in flannel and jeans who had a big smile on his face. He greeted Dee and me with a warm hello. All that kept going through my head initially was, *How come I've met so many Bozos? Jesus, send me a Boaz.* Jill interrupted my thought, "Why don't you take a ride with Keith?"

Before I knew it, I was sitting in the green monster plowing through thousands of cornstalks, watching the machine strip them of their treasure. I was thrilled and asked Keith all kinds of questions. (For a moment I wanted to live on a farm—but I knew I loved the Hyatt and the Hilton too much.) The sun was going down, and all through my time in the cornfields, I kept thinking about planting, sowing, and reaping, and other things God talks about. It will always be a sweet memory.

We got back to the house, and "Ruth" had prepared a lovely dinner for all of us. Boaz sat at the table, fresh and showered, ready to enjoy a feast after a long, hard day's work. It wasn't long before I saw how devoted and how in love Jill and Keith were. As the night came to a close, I was so thankful that I experienced, in the flesh, what God feels for each of us. What an amazing Kinsman-Redeemer we have.

Jill's second husband, Keith, and Ruth's second husband, Boaz, rescued them, not out of duty but out of love. Mike Mason captures the romance of Ruth when he explains,

> Boaz—this elder, avuncular, bourgeois landowner who, though related to Ruth, has no more reason to take notice of her than to fly to the moon—this man actually falls head over heels in love with a poor and alien peasant girl! . . .
>
> The moral of the story is that this is exactly how our Lord feels toward us. Although there is no reason on earth why the great King of the Universe should look twice at this petty, filthy breed of grasshoppers called mankind, nevertheless He says to us, "You have stolen my heart, my sister, my bride; you have stolen my heart with one glance of your eyes" (Song 4:9 NIV). Imagine— we have stolen the heart of God! And this same awesome, awestruck God turns out to be our very own next-of-kin, our long-lost rich relative, the one person who happens to be closer to us than anybody else and who is bound to us inextricably—not only by a blood covenant, but also, astoundingly, by the simple fact of His profoundly genuine love for us.[7]

1. Give a brief summary of each of the following passages:
   A. Ruth 1:1–5

   _____

   _____

   B. Ruth 1:6–9

   _____

   _____

   C. Ruth 1:15–16

   _____

   _____

2. In Ruth 2 we meet Boaz, the *go'el,* the kinsman-redeemer. Describe him, according to the following passages in Ruth, and then see if you can discover how he is a reflection of our Redeemer, Jesus.
   A. Ruth 2:1

   _____

   _____

How does this reflect Jesus?

_____

_____

B. Ruth 2:8

_____

_____

How does this reflect Jesus?

_____

_____

C. Ruth 4:9–10

_____

_____

How does this reflect Jesus?

_____

_____

3. The idea of *exchange* is important in the portrait of *The Redeemer.* Ruth was an outcast, a widow, in poverty, and barren. What did Boaz give her in exchange for each?

_____

_____

_____

This portrait of Boaz rescuing Ruth as her *go'el* is similar to the portrait of Hosea rescuing Gomer. Walter Wangerin, in *The Book of God: The Bible as a Novel,* tells the story like this:

> There was in Israel a prophet named Hosea who married a woman named Gomer. In the early years of their marriage she bore her husband three children. . . . But after they had grown into stout youths, Gomer suddenly gathered her things and ran away from her house, her husband, and her family.
>
> She took a lover. She descended into harlotry. Soon she was possessed by another man as a slave is possessed by a master. . . .
>
> And to Hosea himself, the Lord said: "Go again and love the woman who has become an adulterer with another man. Love her, Hosea, even as I the Lord love the people of Israel, though they have turned to other gods."
>
> So Hosea bought his wife back again for fifteen shekels of silver and a measure of barley.
>
> And he said to her, "You must live faithfully to me. You cannot belong to another man anymore. And I will be faithful to you."

So he took her back again and loved her. . . .

"O Israel! I will betroth you to me in righteousness and justice, in steadfast
love and in mercy.

"For I have pity on Not Pitied!

"And I say to Not My People, no! You are my people!

"Please answer me now. Please say unto me, 'You are our God'." [8]

Read Hosea 3.

4.   What similarities do you see between Boaz as a redeemer and Hosea as a redeemer? What
differences?

_____

_____

_____

Day 3

My Redeemer Is Faithful and True

Sing some songs about your Redeemer. Continue your memory work.

In an intensely personal account, too painful for elaboration, Hosea told of "buying" back his
adulterous wife (Hosea 3). You must read between the lines to see the hurt and humiliation in Hosea
and also in Gomer. Her false lover was done with her and was selling her on the slave market. Can
you imagine her shame? In chains, naked, exposed—men were looking her over, bidding on her.
Her head was bowed when she heard a familiar, gentle voice. *It's Hosea.* She looked up to see the face
of the husband she had so betrayed.

Gomer's story has similarities to Ruth's, but one important difference is that Gomer is the personification of infidelity, whereas Ruth is the personification of fidelity. Yet the Lord loved them both, not
because of their character but because of His. We are unfaithful, but He is faithful. We are fickle, but
He is true. We are unworthy, but He is worthy.

Up until now we have looked at this story primarily from Hosea's perspective, but it is also important that we understand Gomer's viewpoint. Gomer represents not only unfaithful Israel and the corporate bride of Christ but also you and me. As Derek Kidner says, "Israel's sin is also humanity's and
everyman's."[9] Some of you, like the woman in Francine Rivers's novel *Redeeming Love,* had a hard start
in life. Abused and neglected, you found that sin in the world made you its prisoner. But even those
of us who were blessed with loving Christian parents have experienced the slavery of sin. Jesus said,
"Most assuredly, I say to you, whoever commits sin is a slave of sin" (John 8:34).

We have all been deceived, allured into a trap. The lovers we thought would comfort us have turned on us. We all need to be freed from our chains. A price had to be paid by someone who cared enough to do that. Hosea paid with silver and barley, but Jesus paid with His life to set us free.

1. Read Hosea 3:1.
   A. What command did the Lord give to Hosea in verse 1?

   _____

   _____

Some see in this verse that Hosea was to love his wife "again," meaning she had run off more than once. They interpret the "lover" in this verse as "another one," or as J. B. Phillips paraphrases it, as "an evil man." Others believe this is a flashback to when Hosea originally bought Gomer for a bride price. The New American Standard Bible (NASB) translates verse 1 as "a woman who is loved by her husband," meaning Hosea. Those who hold to this interpretation see the importance of realizing that though Gomer and her counterpart, Israel, were about to experience great discipline, their Husband, or God, still loved them. But in either case, the essence of the verse is the same. The bride is in slavery, and the husband must pay a price to free her, whether it is for the first time or whether it is "again."

   B. So often sin seems attractive at first but then turns on us. How have you experienced this personally? What has happened in your life when you have seen God forgive "again"?

   _____

   _____

   C. To whom did the Lord compare Gomer in verse 1? What similarities existed?

   _____

   _____

What a contrast! God was loving Israel to the uttermost, and she was giving her heart for raisin cakes! The raisin cakes were part of the sexual orgy for the Baal gods. Derek Kidner puts it like this: "The bride, it seems, is only here, or anywhere else, for the cakes and ale."[10]

   D. For what trivial enticements have you chosen to leave the pure light of God?

   _____

   _____

   E. Think about the last couple of days. Think about the different ways you stepped into darkness, and see if you can articulate the lies you allowed yourself to believe.

   _____

   _____

   F. What secret for freedom did Jesus give in John 8:31–32?

   _____

   _____

G. As you think about the lies you tend to believe when you wander after "raisin cakes," what truth from Scripture could you prepare to counteract those lies?

_____

_____

2. Read Hosea 3:2.
    A. What did Hosea need to pay to free his wife?

    _____

    _____

    B. Describe, according to Exodus 21:32, the kind of slave this purchased. What do you think is the significance of this?

    _____

    _____

The small price Hosea paid for Gomer may represent her abject condition, the parallel to our slavery, and also the fact that Hosea was not going to indulge his adulterous wife until he knew her repentance was genuine. This is true love. On a corporate level, though God loved Israel and was going to remain faithful to her, He was not going to indulge her but instead discipline her. She would be going into exile with only the basic necessities.

3. Read Hosea 3:3.
    A. What command and information did Hosea give to Gomer?

    _____

    _____

Robert Chisholm gives strong supporting evidence for interpreting verse 3 to mean that she was to abstain from any further adulterous relationships and that during this time Hosea would commit himself to her care.[11] She would experience both pain and discipline (as Israel was going to), but also during that time the love of the bridegroom-redeemer would be steadfast.

    B. When God is testing us to see if our repentance is genuine, His love is steadfast, though He may allow our life circumstances to be difficult. How is this more loving than indulging us?

    _____

    _____

    C. When Hosea said, at the end of verse 3, "So, too, will I be toward you," what do you think he meant?

    _____

    _____

Just as Hosea was asking her to refrain from sexual relations with others, he was going to refrain from sexual relations with her. He had bought her not for his own pleasure but to reform her. One day, he would be a husband to her again, but not then. John Calvin puts it like this: "I pledge my faith to thee, or, I subscribe myself as thy husband: but another time must be looked for; I yet defer my favour, and suspend it until thou givest proof of true repentance."[12]

Sometimes, when we abstain from a sin, we expect the Lord's favor to come immediately rushing in. When it does not, when we still sense a "distance" from Him, we may get discouraged and return to the sin. This is not true repentance. This is repenting because we do not like the consequences of the sin rather than sorrow for offending the Lord we love. If our repentance is genuine, we will continue to abstain, even if God does not immediately indulge us with His favor, His presence, or His lifting of the difficulty of our circumstances.

The sexual analogy that God used in Hosea is meaningful, for the sexual relationship between husband and wife is the most intimate form of "knowing." This shows us that God indeed longs for intimacy with us but will hold back His sweet and tender presence until He sees consistent evidence that our love is genuine.

> D. Have you experienced a difficult period abstaining from an addictive sin, when you suffered but then later felt the care of Jesus? If you are willing, share briefly.
>
> _____
>
> _____

> 4. How do you respond when you've made a turn and still don't sense the presence of God?
>
> _____
>
> _____
>
> _____

> 5. Read Hosea 3:4–5.
>   A. Hosea was no longer talking to his wife but directly to Israel. List the things they would be going without, according to verse 4.
>
>   _____
>
>   _____

In Hosea's time, Israel would no longer have her own king; Assyria would overtake her. Israel, as an adulterous wife, had mixed worship of pagan gods with their worship of the one true Lord. Some of the things Hosea listed, such as the ephod and sacrifice, were used in true worship, but other things, such as the pillar (shrines to idols) and the teraphim (household gods) were abominably pagan. The *Word Biblical Commentary* explains,

> Israel, in its syncretism, had mixed the holy with the forbidden—had adulterated its religion. So, orthodox and heterodox features alike would now be taken away. Neither leadership, nor worship, nor divination would any longer be available to Israel's citizens.[13]

B. Read Jeremiah 29:10–14. Find details about the length of Israel's deprivation and the attitude of the Lord toward her, even as He deprived her.

_____

_____

C. What change would eventually occur in God's people (Hosea 3:5)?

_____

_____

"David" in this verse refers to Christ, who is "the Root and Offspring of David" (Revelation 22:16). James Montgomery Boice believes this verse is a strong indication that there will be a regathering of Israel and a national repentance of Israel in those last days that are yet to come.[14]

Day 4
Worthy Is the Lamb

Pray praises through the following passage:

And they sang a new song, saying:

> *"You are worthy to take the scroll,*
> *And to open its seals;*
> *For You were slain,*
> *And have redeemed us to God by Your blood*
> *Out of every tribe and tongue and people and nation,*
> *And have made us kings and priests to our God;*
> *And we shall reign on the earth."*

Then I looked, and I heard the voice of many angels around the throne, the living creatures, and the elders; and the number of them was ten thousand times ten thousand, and thousands of thousands, saying with a loud voice:

> *"Worthy is the Lamb who was slain*
> *To receive power and riches and wisdom,*
> *And strength and honor and glory and blessing!"* (Revelation 5:9–12)

Boaz paid with silver and gold to redeem his wife; Hosea paid with a few coins and bushels of barley to redeem his wife; but our Lord paid with His own precious blood to redeem His wife, "the bride of the Lamb" (see Revelation 21:9). James Montgomery Boice parallels our situation with Gomer's:

We are the slave sold on the auction block of sin. . . . But when all seemed lost, God sent the Lord Jesus Christ, his Son, into the marketplace to buy us at the close of his life. If you can understand it as an illustration, God was the auctioneer. He said, "What am I bid for these poor, hopeless, enslaved sinners?"

Jesus said, "I bid the price of my blood."

The Father said, "Sold to the Lord Jesus Christ for the price of his blood." There was no greater bid than that.

So we became his, and he took us and clothed us, not with the dirty robes of our old unrighteousnesses, which are as filthy rags, but with the robes of his righteousness.[15]

Christ is indeed our Redeemer. The portrait of our Redeemer as a Lamb foreordained before "the creation of the world" (1 Peter 1:20 NIV) flows from Genesis through Revelation. Charles Spurgeon said,

The more you read the Bible, and the more you meditate upon it, the more you will be astonished with it. . . . You will find the Scriptures enlarge as you enter them. . . . One of the most interesting points of the Scriptures is their constant tendency to display Christ; and perhaps one of the most beautiful figures under which Jesus Christ is ever exhibited in sacred writ, is the Passover Paschal Lamb.[16]

The very *first* time Jesus appeared on the scene, John the Baptist said, "Behold! The Lamb of God who takes away the sin of the world!" (John 1:29).

God's sovereign plan was in place from the beginning and is evident throughout history. How amazing that Jesus's condemnation in Jerusalem began "the very time" that Passover lambs were beginning to be slaughtered! Darrell Bock explains,

Jesus' condemnation occurs at noon on the day before the Passover (19:14), at the very time the priests were beginning to slaughter the Passover lambs in the temple.

While he was on the cross, "hyssop" was used to give Jesus a sponge of wine (19:29), and hyssop was also used to smear the blood of the Passover lamb on the doorposts in Exodus 12:22.

Furthermore, John 19:36 sees a fulfillment of Scripture in that none of Jesus' bones were broken, and according to Exodus 12:46 no bone of the Passover lamb was to be broken.[17]

Inspired by Spurgeon's beautiful sermons, let's look at the first Passover.

The Bound Lamb

Francisco de Zubarán
(about 1598–1664)

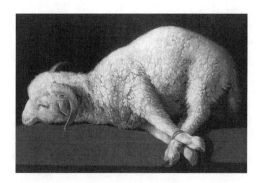

What a night of terror and wonder. Imagine you had lived then. The sun is setting and your husband brings in a lamb, a male in his prime without blemish. You all watch him intently, sensing his solemnity as he checks the lamb with great care. He tells your eldest son to get a basin to collect the blood when he stabs the lamb with a knife. He takes a thick branch of hyssop and dips it in the basin of blood. When he smears it over and on either side of the door, your youngest asks, "Why are you doing this, Father? What does this mean?"

He replies, "This is a clear sign for the Lord to see. Tonight the angel of death will come and strike, but do not fear, for we are safe. We are under the blood of the lamb." You prepare the Passover meal, roasting the lamb, taking pains not to break any bones. Your family sits down to the meal: the lamb, the unleavened bread, and the bitter herbs. Your husband gives a blessing, his voice filled with gratitude and emotion.

When he looks up, joy is in his face. "We will not work as slaves tomorrow. Son, you will not feel that whip on your back ever again. Daughter, you will never be abused again by our cruel taskmaster. My darling wife, we will all soon be free!"

You are dressed to flee, with sandals, a pack of clothes on your back, and a walking stick. Suddenly a shriek pierces the still night. Then another. Soon you hear weeping and wailing everywhere outside. The Egyptians come, pounding on your door, *pleading* with you to leave. A mother is cradling the body of her son in her arms. The grieving father says, "If you do not leave, we shall all be dead!" It is still dark, but you leave quickly, joining the thousands of Israelites in exodus.[18]

1. What emotions and thoughts might you have had if you were a mother or a child that first Passover night?

   _____

   _____

   _____

2. Read Exodus 12.
   A. What was Moses to tell the congregation of Israel in verses 3–4? What were they to do if their family was too small to eat all of one lamb?

   _____

   _____

The Slaying of the Firstborn

GUSTAVE DORÉ
(ABOUT 1598–1664)

Charles Spurgeon says the Israelites were not just to look at the lamb but were actually to eat it, and eat all of it. The parallel that he sees is that we are not just to look at Christ but to allow Him to feed us, and to take all of Him, not part of Him.

B. Where in your life do you feel that you can "take in" more of Jesus? Where have you not allowed Him to feed you?

_____

_____

C. What instructions did the Lord give concerning the lamb in verses 5–10?

_____

_____

The house was marked with three crimson streaks. No blood was put upon the threshold. Woe unto the man that tramples upon the blood of Christ, and treats it as an unholy thing![19]

D. Paul called Christ "our Passover lamb" (1 Corinthians 5:7 NIV). What parallels can you see between Jesus and the lamb in the verses you just read?

_____

_____

E. Why do you think some people are uncomfortable with the emphasis in Christianity on the blood?

_____

_____

F. How were the Israelites to dress and why (Exodus 12:11)? Considering what they had endured, what emotions do you think they might have had?

_____

_____

G. Whom would the Lord strike that night and why (Exodus 12:12)?

_____

_____

H. What would God do to the Egyptian gods?

_____

_____

I. What significance do you see in the statement "I am the Lord"? (v. 12).

_____

_____

J. Remembering that a redeemer rescues and gives something in exchange for the life of the one in bondage, explain how the Passover lamb, both the literal lamb and Christ, our Passover Lamb, filled the role of redeemer.

_____

_____

3. Read 1 Peter 1:13–21.
   A. What instruction did Peter give us in verse 13?

   _____

   _____

"Gird up the loins of your mind" is similar to our "Roll up your sleeves." It reminds us what the Israelites were to do: dress in preparation to flee. We, too, must be prepared, not in our dress, but in our minds—to flee, flee, flee the chains and slavery of sin.

B. How are we to live, according to verses 14–17?

_____

_____

C. Why, according to verses 18–19?

_____

_____

D. How can you personally apply these passages?

_____

_____

E. For how long had Christ been ordained to be our Redeemer, our "Passover lamb" (v. 20)?

_____

_____

4. The portrait of Christ as the Lamb occurs repeatedly in John's vision in the book of Revelation. Read Revelation 5.

A. In verses 5–6, John saw two contrasting portraits of Christ. What were they, and what do you associate with each?

_____

_____

B. None of the powerful figures of Revelation 4 was worthy to open the scroll, and John wept. Who *was* worthy to open the scroll and why (vv. 6–10)?

_____

_____

C. How are we redeemed (v. 9)?

_____

_____

D. Describe the redeemed of Christ and what she will be doing (vv. 9–10)?

_____

_____

5. Read Revelation 21:21–27 for a description of the New Jerusalem, the final resting place of believers.

A. Who will be the source of light?

_____

_____

B. Who will live in this glorious place (v. 27)?

_____

_____

C. Are you written in the Lamb's Book of Life? Explain.

_____

_____

Not only does Christ redeem us from the penalty of sin, but also He is redeeming us from the power of sin. We will look at this important lesson tomorrow.

You Are My Hiding Place

Not only do we need to be redeemed from the penalty of sin, but the power of sin. Meditate on this passage:

> *For in my inner being I delight in God's law; but I see another law at work in the members of my body, waging war against the law of my mind and making me a prisoner of the law of sin at work within my members. What a wretched man I am! Who will rescue me from this body of death? Thanks be to God—through Jesus Christ our Lord!* (Romans 7:22–25 NIV)

Be still before Him. This prayer will help prepare you for day 5:

> Oh Lord, I can't do it. Every time I try, I fail. Who will rescue me? I know You will! Just as You rescued me from the penalty of sin, You, not I, can deliver me from its terrible power. When temptation calls, send me running to You, to bury my head in Your chest. There, let Your mind renew my mind and allow Your strength to flow into my weakness. Thanks be to God, through Jesus, my Lord.

(Dee) For many years I thought the way to overcome the power of sin was to read my Bible more, pray more, and so on. The problem with my thinking was that though those disciplines are critical to my spiritual health, I was still trusting that *I* could do it—and you know what? *I* can't. I can't overcome the power of sin any more than I can overcome the penalty of sin. It has to be Jesus.

So what is the solution? There's a story in *Prince Caspian,* from C. S. Lewis's Narnia series, that gives insight. The great lion, Aslan (who represents Jesus) has asked Lucy to do something difficult.

> "Do you mean that is what you want me to do?" gasped Lucy.
>
> ". . . It is hard for you, little one," said Aslan. . . .
>
> Lucy buried her head in his mane to hide from his face. But there must have been some magic in his mane. She could feel lion-strength going into her. Quite suddenly she sat up.
>
> "I'm sorry, Aslan," she said, "I'm ready now."
>
> "Now you are a lioness," said Aslan.[20]

Do you see? The secret isn't in what I can do, but in what the mighty power of Christ can do through me. The reason we are so excited about the whole concept of falling in love with Jesus is that our love relationship is the key to strength. We must "bury our faces in His mane" and keep them there until we sense "lion-strength" going into us. Surely, spending time with Him in His Word and in prayer does deepen our love relationship with Him, but it's a critical difference to remember to rely on His power instead of our own. When we "bury our faces in His mane," when we "are still, and know that He is God," He reminds us of His love and gives us the faith to submit, not to the flesh but to the Spirit. Each time we do that, more "lion-strength" grows in us, helping us defeat the old nature.

We're going to study some critical passages in Romans 6–8 today that consider how Christ delivers from the power of sin. Paul had just explained that the law cannot deliver; it can only show us how far short we fall of God's holy standard. He also showed us that a tremendous battle is going on in every believer. This is because we have a "new nature" in Christ, but the old nature of sin, that snarling beast, is still alive and kicking, desiring to reclaim the territory he has lost.

1. Read Romans 7:14–25.
    A. How did Paul describe the law and then himself in verse 14? What did he mean?

    _____

    _____

When Gomer returned to her sin, she returned to her chains. In the same way, when we sin, we allow the old nature to reclaim territory, to loop the chains over us again.

    B. Describe the battle raging within, according to verses 15–21.

    _____

    _____

    C. Describe the two natures fighting within each believer, according to verses 22–23.

    _____

    _____

While the unregenerate man may have pricks of conscience, he is not going to experience the same battle as the man who has the Spirit of Christ in him. He is more likely, therefore, to rush headlong into sin.

    D. Take a specific area you often battle within, such as what you say, what you watch, what you think, or what you eat. Describe what the "inward man" (v. 22), the new spiritual nature, might think and do and what the old nature might think and do.

    _____

    _____

    E. What was Paul's cry in verse 24?

    _____

    _____

F. What is the answer for being redeemed from our slavery to the power of sin, according to verse 25?

_____

_____

Imagine these two natures fighting within your heart. The nature of Christ is indeed the stronger, and the old nature has been severely wounded, but it is trying to recapture its lost domain. Each time you give in to it, it regains territory and strength, but each time you, by faith, submit to the Spirit of Christ, that new nature gains strength.

2. What strategy can we use to feed and strengthen the new nature, according to Romans 6:11–14?

_____

_____

_____

3. What strategy can we use to strengthen the new nature, according to Romans 8:5–8?

_____

_____

_____

4. What strategy does Romans 8:13 give us?

_____

_____

_____

5. When we cry out to God for help, not even knowing how to pray, what comfort can we find in Romans 8:26–27?

_____

_____

_____

Redemption from the power of sin will not be complete until we see Jesus face to face with our new sanctified bodies. But, through faith, we can see the new nature grow stronger and the old nature weaker. John Calvin tells us not to despond because we have not wholly crucified the flesh: "For this work of God is not completed in the day in which it is begun in us; but it gradually goes on, and by daily advances is brought by degrees to its end."[21]

We have considered Jesus as the Lamb of God this week. This Lamb is not always gentle. In Revelation, John saw in a vision men pleading with the mountains to fall on them to hide them from "the wrath of the Lamb!" (Revelation 6:16). Just as the Lamb is hidden in the Lion, the Lion is hidden in the Lamb. We will concentrate on the Lion, as the writings of John and Hosea portray Him, next week.

Review

Were you "kissed" by the King this week? If so, how?

Prayer Time

Break into groups of three to intercede for one another about breaking the power of sin. Each woman should take a turn lifting up her own need, either by naming her area of struggle specifically, such as, "Lord, I am anxious and lacking in Your peace," or "I am tempted by sexual immorality," or simply saying, "I lift up my area of weakness." Then the others can pray sentence prayers. Remember to concentrate on praying for Christ's strength, Christ's mind, Christ's peace to flow into one another. Here are some ideas:

> "Please help Amy bury her face in Your mane throughout the day, drawing on Your strength."

> "Please help Amy be still and cast her cares on You. Remind her of Your care for her."

> "Please help Amy to offer her body not to sin but to You."

> "Please renew Amy's mind with Your mind, Amy's strength with Your strength."

Next week you will be in the same groups for accountability and continued prayer.

The Lion
Artist: Martin French (www.martinfrench.com)

Week 8
THE LION

So I will be to them like a lion; Like a leopard by the road I will lurk; I will meet them like a bear deprived of her cubs; I will tear open their rib cage, and there I will devour them like a lion. The wild beast shall tear them.

—HOSEA 13:7–8

MEMORY VERSE:
HEBREWS 12:28–29

*Y*ou are not likely to find this Scripture passage crocheted on a cushion or painted on a plaque. The verses we like to display are the ones about His unfailing love, His mercy, and His care.

Likewise, we are drawn to the portraits of the Lord that show His gentle side: a Bridegroom betrothing His bride, a Father teaching His child to walk, and a Redeemer rescuing us. But unless we *also* see the portraits of Jesus that show His holiness and just wrath, we are living in a fantasy world and will fail to mature as we so desperately need to. After speaking about the great sin of turning away from the Lord, the author of Hebrews warned us to "serve God acceptably with reverence and godly fear" (12:28). Why? Because, he wrote, "*Our God is a consuming fire*" (12:29).

The first principle of the wisdom literature of the Bible is that the fear of the Lord is the beginning of wisdom. But after He relieves our fears of hell, we often move into a time, in our immaturity, when we fail to revere Him as we ought. In *Your God Is Too Small*, J. B. Phillips says that we want to reduce God so that we can control Him, making Him a policeman or an indulgent grandfather. But the God of the universe cannot be contained. Even after He has relieved our fears of hell, we need to fear dishonoring His name.

Sometimes we wonder how our almighty God feels about the flippant bumper stickers, gaudy T-shirts, and trite trinkets in the marketplace that bear His holy name. (Or how the person wearing the T-shirt or bearing the bumper sticker may disgrace Him with his or her behavior.) Because He is a God of grace, when we make choices that lack reverence, He doesn't routinely cut us down with bolts of lightning but allows us to mature and understand His majesty and holiness.

(*Kathy*) I was a very young believer in Jesus when I started singing about Him. Because of the new and exciting thrill of knowing Him and being loved by Him, songs were just pouring out of me. I wasn't an accomplished guitar player and pianist, but with the few chords I knew on both of those instruments, I wrote a lot. In that season I was taking in so much I couldn't help but let it out.

I was such a novice at songwriting that the songs were either epics that told His story from

Genesis to Revelation (in one song), or quite cute, lighthearted, and playful. Nonetheless, people seemed to enjoy them, and I enjoyed singing them.

I remember reading a little poem comparing God to commercial slogans. I thought it would be fun to put it to music. It ended up having three chords and a title of "God Is Like Pepsi." (Hang in there with me—I'll explain.) I'm probably dating myself, but some of you may remember . . .

> God is like Ford—
>> He has the better idea.

> God is like Coke—
>> He is the real thing.

> God is like Pan Am—
>> He makes the going great.

> God is like Right Guard—
>> So why should you sweat it?

Okay, I am really embarrassed now. The chorus said something like this:

> God is like Pepsi—

> He's got a lot to give

> for He sent His only Son

> so that you and I could live . . .

When I sang at little coffeehouses and churches where I'd been before, people screamed out, "Sing the Pepsi song!" (My audiences apparently lacked maturity as well!)

Then I was asked to sing at an Episcopal church in Connecticut. I remember really enjoying the service. A visiting pastor from Romania gave the message. It was powerful and poignant. I sang through my usual set and again got great laughter and applause from the "Pepsi generation." At the end of the service, through all the hubbub of meeting and greeting, the missionary gently tapped me on the shoulder and asked if he could speak to me. I was anticipating a response like the ones I was getting from others—

"You were wonderful."

"You are so gifted."

"You really blessed me."

"God's going to take you places."

The missionary looked in my eyes intently. What came out of his mouth has stayed with me since that day. It has also deeply affected my awareness of the holiness of God and the call on His people.

"Miss Troccoli, where I am living and ministering, there is great suffering. There are deep cries of prayer to the Father, and they are holding on to His promises for their very lives. I cannot see my people dying for a God that is like Dial soap."

I was a little shocked, to say the least. But it was so full of the truth. In no way could I refute it, ignore it, or deny it. I never sang the song again.

Many of the portraits painted of Jesus show Him as gentle and mild—even effeminate, as if the artist wanted to strip Him of His power, His holy and righteous indignation, and His strength. Others have claimed that the God of the Old Testament is full of wrath, but the God of the New Testament is gentle and mild. Not so. "Jesus Christ is the same yesterday, today, and forever" (Hebrews 13:8). The anger we see in Hosea is the same anger we see when He overturned the tables of the money changers in John. He does not want us to forget Him or fail to fear Him. He has been, is now, and will be seeking true worshipers who love Him with all their hearts, souls, and minds.

VIDEO NOTES FOR WEEK 8

Don't cover these questions in discussion. Watch the video first, and then put your chairs in a circle to discuss this lesson.

1. "So I will be to them like a _____;

   Like a leopard by the road I will_____

   I will meet them like a bear _____ _____ _____ _____;

   I will tear open their _____ _____,

   And there I will devour them like a _____.

   The wild beast shall tear them." (Hosea 13:7–8)

2. The first principle of the wisdom literature in the Bible is _____ _____ ____ ____ _____ is the beginning of wisdom.

These were not empty threats to Israel:

- Early in the eighth century BC, the northern kingdom fell.

- The southern kingdom was invaded by the Assyrians some years after.

3. Though God will discipline His people, it grieves Him to do so. You can see His heart in Hosea:

"I taught Ephraim to _____, taking them by the arms" (11:3).

"How can I _____ _____ _____, Ephraim?" (11:8).

4. But one day "They shall walk after the LORD. He will roar like a lion. When He roars, then His sons shall _____ _____ from the west" (Hosea 11:10).

4. Jesus said to Pilate, "Therefore the one who delivered Me to you has the _____ sin. (John 19:11).

5. Our point is not to trivialize sin but to focus on what is most important so that the rest will _____ _____ _____.

6. The greatest commandment is to_____

7. So we must
   • fear dishonoring Him,

   • fear f_____ Him,

   • fear unf_____.

Otherwise, He may need to be a Lion in your life to bring you to your senses, to bring you trembling home.

WARM UP

What do you know about lions? (If your closest exposure is a housecat, zoologists say there are similarities!) Describe their double nature. Why do you think the lion is considered the king of the jungle?

What do you particularly remember from the video? Why?

INTRODUCTION QUESTIONS

Please cover in your discussion group. These are vital.

1. Why is it important to understand that God is not only loving but also holy?

   _____

   _____

   _____

2. Why do you think the missionary from Romania approached Kathy after she sang "God Is Like Pepsi"?

   _____

   _____

   _____

3. What do you think C. S. Lewis was saying when he described Aslan this way: "He's not safe—but he's good."[1] (If you have experienced this, share when, in just a few words.)

   _____

   _____

   _____

Day 1

Holy, Holy

Seizing the heavy tables filled with coins, overturning them on the stone floor, slashing a whip through the air, Jesus terrified the crowd. Tables fell, coins clattered, lambs bleated, birds squawked, and people cried out. John described the scene:

> *Now the Passover of the Jews was at hand, and Jesus went up to Jerusalem. And He found in the temple those who sold oxen and sheep and doves, and the money changers doing business. When He had made a whip of cords, He drove them all out of the temple, with the sheep and the oxen, and poured out the changers' money and overturned the tables.* (John 2:13–15)

This was the first time Jesus cleared the temple, during a Passover early in His ministry. John's primary point, as is typical of his gospel, is that Jesus *was* God and therefore had the authority to cleanse the courts of the money changers, of the noise, of the animals that were wandering into the temple itself and defecating. Jesus was protecting those who longed to worship. It was a bold and astonishing act, and it frightened the crowd. Leon Morris wrote, "It was not so much the physical force as the moral power" that terrified the crowd.[2]

Later, Jesus cleared the temple *again*, and Matthew, Mark, and Luke recorded that cleansing. That time was after His triumphal entry on what we call Palm Sunday. It was the terrible eve of the

Passover on which He would offer Himself as the perfect Lamb of God.[3] The first cleansing shocked the religious leaders, but the second sealed their determination to destroy Jesus.[4]

Neither cleansing was an impulsive act. Our Lord's wrath is different from man's. He never "loses it," but He does become angry. As John White points out, Jesus *made* the whip Himself. "His act of enraged violence was premeditated . . . he made a plan and carried it out."[5]

We need to ask ourselves, *What was it that made God so angry in the books of Hosea and John?* It is interesting, for the sin was similar.

1. Jesus had just performed His first miracle. What was it, and how did it show that God was looking for a new kind of relationship with His people (John 2:1–12)?

   _____

   _____

   _____

2. Read John 2:13–17. Describe the scene, finding all the details you can.

   _____

   _____

   _____

3. One of several places the Bible records prophecies of this incident is in Malachi 3:1–7. Read it.
   A. How did Malachi describe Jesus (v. 1), and what did he say He would do?

      _____

      _____

   B. What pictures did Malachi paint of Jesus (vv. 2–3), and what qualities do they have in common with *The Lion?*

      _____

      _____

   C. What were some of the sins that provoked His wrath (vv. 4–5)? What is the root sin?

      _____

      _____

   D. What did the Lord say about Himself in Malachi 3:6?

      _____

      _____

Notice the "I am," which is like the "I AMs" of Exodus and John. Another implication of "I AM" is that He is the same—not "I WAS" or "I WILL BE," but "I AM." The anger we see in Hosea is the same anger we see in John. He does not want us to forget Him, to fail to fear Him, or to use Him. He has been, is now, and will be seeking true worshipers who love Him with all their hearts, souls, and minds.

E. Explain why the teaching that the Lord is a God of wrath in the Old Testament who changes to a God of mercy in the New Testament is erroneous.

_____

_____

4. Jesus cleared the money changers from the temple because they were preventing God's people from truly worshiping. The noise of braying animals and bargaining money changers corrupted the worship. Those who were turning God's house into a marketplace simply didn't revere the Lord. How is this similar to the sin Israel committed in Hosea ("but Me she forgot")?

_____

_____

_____

Though it pleases God when we understand His great love for us and run into His arms, we must never, ever forget that He is holy, awesome, and above all gods. This is His character throughout Scripture. Just as in Hosea, just as in John, the Lord today longs for us to fear and to love Him. How often we forget His holiness!

- It is not hidden from the Lord Almighty when our worship or our ministry is more about glorifying ourselves than glorifying Him.

- It is not a small thing to a holy God when, because we have failed to fear and to love Him, that we are grumbling, gossiping, and sowing discord among brothers.

- It is not unnoticed by the Creator of heaven and earth when we, because of our neglect of Him, are running to the gods of worldly pleasures to fill up our souls.

5. In what areas do you feel you may be disregarding the holiness of the Lord?

_____

_____

_____

6. Read John 2:18–21.
   A. What question did the Jews ask and why (v. 18)?

_____

_____

The religious leaders were shocked by this bold act and demanded to know on what authority Jesus acted. The sign He mentioned, which they did not understand, was the sign of the Resurrection. Of course Jesus had the authority! He was God.

B. How did Jesus respond? Who did they think He meant, and what did He really mean (John 2:19–21)?

_____

_____

Bock explains this first cleansing by Jesus is "seen in messianic terms as a purifying act to get the temple ready for a new era." It is a fulfillment of several prophecies, including Psalm 69:9, where zeal for His Father's house would consume Him. That same zeal would have Him cleanse the temple again, just before His death. "Not only does it consume his action now, but that devotion and single-minded dedication will lead to Jesus' death. Jesus' concern is for true, pure, worship (John 4:24)."[6]

7. What do you learn from this portrait of Jesus in the gospel of John concerning His character and passions? How will you apply this to your life?

_____

_____

_____

Day 2

Open the Eyes of My Heart, Lord

"Open the Eyes of My Heart" is a good prayer to sing with your whole heart before beginning study. Then have a sense of anticipation.

Begin your memory work.

One of the characteristics we have come to love about truly godly friends is that they *do* see their continual need, for they are in the presence of God's light. When Dee's daughter Sally went to Covenant Seminary in St. Louis, she told of how open the other students were about their sin. "So often," Sally said, "I have been to prayer groups where we concentrated on praying for the needs of friends and family members, but at Covenant, I was blown away by the personal vulnerability." There she heard requests like these:

> "I'm so full of pride—I hate it. Pray I will humble myself before God chooses to do it for me!"

> "I get so jealous of students who have more than I do—pray I will die to that rottenness and that contentment will live."

"I am so selfish—all through the day, my thoughts are primarily about myself. Pray for me, please."

One pastor suggested that when criticized because of our depravity we should say, "You don't know the half of it!"

1. How would you evaluate your prayer times in this group? Do you feel you are being honest and vulnerable with the others?

    _____

    _____

    _____

2. Why do we need one another in this battle against sin?

    _____

    _____

    _____

We can be thankful that our God is slow to anger. But we must not let His grace lull us into thinking that we can disregard His holiness or that our sin does not grieve Him or that we can relax in our battle. As long as we live in these bodies, we will have a battle with sin. If we do something wrong and nothing happens, we must not conclude that it doesn't matter to God or that we have "gotten away with it."

Human beings have consistently taken advantage of the grace of God. Solomon commented on this in regard to people in the world:

> *Because the sentence against evil deeds is so long in coming, people in general think they can get by with murder.*
>
> *Even though a person sins and gets by with it hundreds of times throughout a long life, I'm still convinced that the good life is reserved for the person who fears God, who lives reverently in his presence, and that the evil person will not experience a "good" life. No matter how many days he lives, they'll all be as flat and colorless as a shadow—because he doesn't fear God.* (Ecclesiastes 8:11–13 MSG)

3. According to Ecclesiastes 3:8, why do men do evil? What is faulty about their thinking?

    _____

    _____

    _____

It isn't just people of the world who think they can get by with murder. We as believers can be full of hatred toward our brothers, persistent in sexual immorality, filled with pride, given over to gluttony, or generally apathetic about our love for God. Why? It may be because God has been gracious to us, and we assume He will always forgive us. Scripture warns against assuming upon grace and becoming apathetic. God will not always strive with us. If we continue in sin, soon we will not even be able to hear His promptings (see Proverbs 2:20–22).

If we fail to look at the whole Word of God, and if we become apathetic about our sin, God may become the Lion to us and seek us out. Not only is this true of the corporate church, but the Lord also chooses to be the Lion in our individual lives. Because of His great love for us, He may chasten us for our sin. When we think we can hide our sin from Him, He may, as Hosea said repeatedly, stalk us like a lion, tear at our very beings, and cause us to fear Him as we ought. When we are in rebellion, we may hide, but the Lion can always hunt us and find us. We may run, but the Lion can always overtake us. We may ignore His still, small voice, but the Lord will roar until we come trembling back.

There is a similarity between Hosea 4 and Romans 1, where Paul condemned the whole world in that "although they knew God, they did not glorify Him" (Romans 1:21). The Gentiles knew God existed because of Creation, yet they *suppressed* the truth about Him so they could do what they wanted to do. The Israelites had more knowledge than just Creation, but they, too, *suppressed* that truth, and for the same reason.

A repeated theme in Hosea is that the people cherished "a spirit of harlotry." They thought they had knowledge of God, but they were selective about their knowledge. They were offering sacrifices and having festivals, but their empty displays of piety only angered God more. In Hosea 4 He took them into court and demanded that they hear how they had broken covenant with Him.

Read Hosea 4:1–5:7.

4. Find the oft-repeated pattern in Scripture when God calls His people together for an important pronouncement. How did He begin? What was the emotion?
   A. Isaiah 1:2–3

   _____

   _____

   B. Amos 3:1–2, 8

   _____

   _____

   C. Hosea 4:1

   _____

   _____

5. What three things did the Israelites lack, according to Hosea 4:1?

   _____

   _____

   _____

6. What covenant-breaking deeds did Hosea list (v. 2)? (Consider how they broke the Ten Commandments.)

_____

_____

_____

7. What is the primary sin as reiterated in Hosea 4:6?

_____

_____

_____

There is this continual tension in Hosea: they were His people, yet they certainly didn't act like His people. They had some knowledge of Him, but they had suppressed whatever they didn't want to know. Their spirit of harlotry had caused them to love their deeds more than Him and to shut out the truths that interfered with those deeds. He must be the Lion in their lives.

8. Describe the "spirit of harlotry" and the Lord's response.
   A. Describe their hearts (Hosea 4:8) and the Lord's response (Hosea 4:9–10).

   _____

   _____

   B. Instead of coming under the shadow of His wings, what did they do, according to Hosea 4:11–13?

   _____

   _____

   C. How did God describe His people in Hosea 4:16a? Because of this, what would He do? What was the picture He painted in Hosea 4:16b?

   _____

   _____

   Jehovah would feed them "as a lamb in a large place," as a lamb unprotected out on the hills, a prey to wolves and lions.[7]

9. What indictment did God repeat in Hosea 5:4?

_____

_____

_____

_____

10. Israel was still making sacrifices with her flocks and herds, still having festivals. But what did God say in Hosea 5:6–7?

_____

_____

_____

They thought those religious festivals would bring blessing, but instead, they brought judgment.

11. How can God's people today delude themselves with religious activity when, in fact, they are far from God? How can you?

_____

_____

_____

12. Are there deeds or thought patterns you are clinging to because you cherish them more than God? Are you ignoring scriptures because you have set your heart on sexual immorality, gluttony, popularity, revenge? Ask God to open the eyes of your heart to any spirit of harlotry, then write down what He shows you. Ask Him to help you trust and obey Him.

_____

_____

_____

Day 3

I Will Be Like a Lion

Worship.

Sing songs of holiness to the Lord.

Some of the great poets have written about Christ as a Lion. For example, in the "The Second Coming," the Irish poet W. B. Yeats wrote of a lion "slouching" toward us, "moving its slow thighs"— powerful images of the king of the beasts ready to pounce.

(Dee) I wrote an essay on Yeats' "The Second Coming" as a student at college, but because I was blind to spiritual truths, I had _no_ idea what he was talking about. Apparently my professor didn't either, for I received an A on my senseless essay. (It makes me laugh to think about it now.)

A beloved American poet, T. S. Eliot, wrote "Gerontion." He expresses the profundity of how the baby, the Word, that was helpless in a womb, is also "Christ the Tiger." Though Jesus came gently into the world, that is not how He will return, as evidenced by Martin French's portrait we see in week 2.

Have you ever heard it said that all sin is the same in God's eyes? It simply isn't so. Even Jesus told Pilate, in speaking of Judas, "The one who delivered Me to you has the greater sin" (John 19:11). So where do we get this erroneous teaching? Sometimes we take true statements, but then, like the person who adds two plus two and gets five, we leap to a false conclusion. It seems that some have thought,

All sin grieves the heart of God. (True)

All sin deserves the sentence of death, so even if you have never robbed a bank or murdered anyone, you still need a Savior. (True)

Therefore, all sin is the same in God's eyes. (False)

Ken Gire says that since the first commandment is to love the Lord your God with all your heart, soul, and mind, it would make sense that what would grieve the Lord the most is to *not* love Him with all your heart, soul, and mind. Would this not be similar to "forgetting" Him, as the people in Hosea's day did?

1. If someone said to you, "All sin is the same in God's eyes," how would you respond?

_____

_____

_____

Often, in our self-righteousness, we can go to church and refrain from smoking and drinking yet grumble and gossip about our brothers. What irony! Since the second greatest commandment is to love our neighbor as ourselves, wouldn't it grieve the Lord deeply when we don't?

2. One sin, Jesus said, is unforgivable. Read Mark 3:20–29.
   A. From whom did the scribes say Jesus received His power (v. 22)?

   _____

   _____

   B. What was illogical about their accusation (v. 23)?

   _____

   _____

   C. What promise and what warning did Jesus give in verses 28–29?

   _____

   _____

Many have worried needlessly that they have committed the "unpardonable sin." Concern in itself shows a tender heart and should let them know they have not done this. When people attributed the power of the Holy Spirit to Satan, they were revealing a hardness in their hearts to the Holy Spirit. When you are hardened toward the Holy Spirit, you cannot repent. If you cannot repent, you cannot be forgiven, and you do not have a lifeline. A person who wants to repent has not committed this sin. Also, anyone who has been born again has received the Holy Spirit and cannot commit this sin because God is not divided against Himself.

3. List the seven sins that are particularly abhorrent to God, according to Proverbs 6:16–19. What do you learn from this list?

   _____

   _____

   _____

4. Examine your own life in light of this list. Be still. What does His Spirit show you?

   _____

   _____

   _____

In Hosea, the Lord certainly became like a lion in the lives of the Israelites. A good part of Hosea is about how God, because of the harlotry of His people, was going to allow them to be captured, torn, and ravaged for many, many years. This was no empty threat, for the prophecy of Hosea was fulfilled when the northern kingdom fell in 722 BC and when the Assyrians invaded the southern kingdom in 701 BC.

To avoid needing attention from the Lion, we need to let the Word teach us—and then we must obey. We should choose our Bible studies carefully. While topical studies have great value, if we do *only* topical studies, it is a bit like doing the easy parts of the puzzle but never seeing the whole picture. We must see the hard parts of God's Word as well and not treat God's Word as a scene from which we choose only the pieces that fit together easily.

It is vital to study *whole books* and to seek churches that preach through whole books. Though it is hard to see Jesus as a Lion, He *is* a Lion, both in our individual lives and in the life of His corporate bride. We as individuals and we as the church *will* suffer, for suffering is part of God's refining plan in the lives of His people. We must be prepared.

5. Read Hosea 5:8–15.
   A. What did God tell Hosea to do in verse 8?

   _____

   _____

   B. What was the indictment against Ephraim in verse 11, and what insect did the Lord say He would be like? What do you think He meant?

_____

_____

First, a moth distracts us or bothers us in a harmless way. . . . God may be saying that at the beginning of our path of disobedience he is like that. He distracts us from sin, bothers us, tries to get us away from it and back to thinking of him once again.

Second, many moths are destructive. . . . Here is a case where we, having resisted the fluttering of the moth, now find it to have gotten into the things we value and to have destroyed them. God says that he will also do that to turn us to him.[8]

C. Have you ever experienced losing something of value and having that pain turn you to God? If so, explain.

_____

_____

D. Instead of repenting when God was "like a moth," what did Ephraim (another name for Israel) do, according to Hosea 5:13?

_____

_____

E. Since God's people persisted in rebellion, what would He be like, according to Hosea 5:14?

_____

_____

F. What is the ultimate goal of God's wrath toward His people (Hosea 5:15)?

_____

_____

Day 4
I Love an Untame Lion

Be still before the Lord. Think of ways He has been faithful to You, and thank Him for those. Sing "Great Is Thy Faithfulness."

Meditate on this passage: "Your love is like the morning mist, like the early dew that disappears" (Hosea 6:4 NIV).

Say this prayer to prepare you for day 4:

O Lord, my love is unfaithful, like the morning mist that disappears when the heat comes. Forgive me. Help me truly repent. Help me be faithful. I cannot do it on my own. Help me abandon myself to Your Spirit, Your strength today. Help my faithfulness become like Yours.

Michelle Tumes, inspired by Aslan in The Chronicles of Narnia, wrote a song called "I Love an Untame Lion." When He roars, her heart hesitates, and she wants to turn and run. Yet how can she resist? He is calling her to a place she's never seen, a place of endless dawn, golden as the sun. The Lion, perhaps more than the other portraits, shows us both the wonderful and terrible sides of God.

Now, in chapters 5—11 of Hosea, a kaleidoscope of pictures portrays the refining judgment of God. The Lord is a lion who seizes and tears; He is a net that falls over a senseless dove; He is One who releases a flood of water on them.

Many believers have grasped the idea of grace but have ignored God's holy anger. Voltaire once said of God, "Forgiveness? That's his job!" One young husband who proclaimed Christ said, when he gave in to drunkenness and infidelity, "God will forgive me. What's the big deal?" James Montgomery Boice says, "We are never in greater danger than when we assume that he will always forgive us as long as we go through the outward forms of repentance."[9]

Continually in Hosea we see a contrast between an unholy and "partially" repentant people and a holy God who will indeed carry out His refining process, not "partially," but completely. By Hosea 11, the people were truly repentant. Instead of flitting like a silly dove between Assyria and Egypt for help, they had had their fill of each and were finally going home to the Father, the Lion. They would return at the sound of His roar, trembling, but thankful to be home.

1. Read Hosea 6:4–6.
   A. What picture does verse 4 give of the faithfulness of the people? What truth does this picture communicate?

   _____

   _____

   B. In what areas is your faithfulness like the morning mist?

   _____

   _____

   C. What verbs did Hosea use in verse 5 to show the action of the sword, the Word of God?

   _____

   _____

   D. What did God long to see in His people, according to verse 6?

   _____

   _____

E. How can you apply this passage to your life?

_____

_____

2. Read Hosea 7:4–9.

A. What picture did Hosea give of the increasing and unrestrained sexual passions of the Israelites in verse 4?

_____

_____

B. One lie of the enemy is that we can get "sin out of our system" by giving in to it: unleashing our anger, indulging in that extra dessert, playing with sexual immorality. Instead, what picture does verse 6 give?

_____

_____

C. How could you apply this truth to your life?

_____

_____

D. Because Ephraim, or God's people, had mixed themselves with the people of other gods, what were they like according to verse 8? What does this picture communicate?

_____

_____

E. Lack of knowledge of God leads to a lack of self-knowledge. How did Hosea picture this in verse 9?

_____

_____

3. In Hosea 7:11–12, to whom was Israel planning to go for help? To what did the Lord compare them? What would be His response?

_____

_____

_____

The dove is reported to be witless and easy to trap. How foolish we are when we think sinful choices can help us and we run to them instead of to God. When we do, God allows us to be trapped.

4. Whether your translation says "eagle" or a "vulture" in 8:1, the picture is of a bird of prey that is going to swoop down on a weakened party. Most believe that vulture to be Assyria.

A. In Hosea 8:1–3, what did God promise and why?

B. This picture also appears in Deuteronomy 28:49. What other details do you see there?

_____

_____

5. When the Lord allows others to come upon us like a vulture, or when He Himself comes upon us like a lion, His purpose is always our true repentance. What picture does Hosea 11:10–11 give?

_____

_____

_____

We do not know which homecoming this passage picture portrays, or if it is repeated elsewhere. Derek Kidner writes:

> It is not easy to know which stage of history is in mind here: whether some intermediate day of the lion's roar, such as the overthrow of Babylon which brought a remnant of Israel (including some from these northern tribes) home to Jerusalem; or the spiritual homecoming of God's "sons" (10b) of many nations in the gospel age (in line with Paul's quotation of Hosea 2:23 and 1:10 in Romans 9:25–26); or again the great turning of the Lord which is predicted in Romans 11:12, 25ff. What is certain is that the final event will far surpass our wisest thoughts and wildest expectations.[10]

Day 5

The Lion King

(Dee) Two weeks after we learned Steve had cancer, our daughter Sally sang "A Mighty Fortress Is Our God" as a solo in church. She wept as she sang, but she sang it as the fighting song it is, and people kept saying, "I never really heard that song before. I never really understood it." It *is* a wonderful song. Think about the spiritual forces of darkness you long to conquer in your life or see conquered in the lives of others. Turn to it in Appendix A, and sing it as a prayer.

Review your memory work.

We love the movie *The Lion King*. While it is definitely a mixture of Christianity and spirituality (a little nature worship, a little Eastern religion), if you sift out the dross, you are left with some golden gospel pictures.

In the opening scene, the whole animal kingdom is coming to worship the lion king and his new-born cub: impalas running, elephants thundering, giraffes loping, and birds soaring—all in great excitement. The lion king stands high on a cliff, the wind blowing his majestic mane, the sun gleaming on him, and all of the animals bow down. Then he proudly holds up his cub, Simba, and the music soars and creation rejoices. It reminds us of the scene in Revelation 5 where all of creation bows down to the Lamb of God.

The lion king reigns over whatever the sun touches, except, as he tells his little Simba, that "area of darkness." (Jesus reigns over *all* principalities, for even Satan must get permission from Him.) The lion king is tough but tender, and fiercely protective of Simba. Simba could easily represent us, as God's erring children. Though Simba wanders into the darkness and experiences great trial, he finally runs home to his father. The father allows Simba to roam and even to be hurt for his own good, but in the end, this lion king will defeat all enemies. As he says reassuringly to Simba: "Nobody messes with your dad."

> *"They shall walk after the LORD.*
> *He will roar like a lion.*
> *When He roars,*
> *Then His sons shall come trembling from the west;*
> *They shall come trembling like a bird from Egypt,*
> *Like a dove from the land of Assyria.*
> *And I will let them dwell in their houses,"*
> *Says the LORD.* (Hosea 11:10–11)

Hosea and John seem to have received similar mysterious visions, both involving a lion, both involving the victory of the Lion of Judah.

1. Read Revelation 5.
   A. Describe the scroll in verse 1, the seals, and in which hand someone was holding it.

   _____

   _____

Though there are many thoughts on what is in this scroll, clearly it contained the mysteries of God, and the number seven symbolizes completeness. The right hand is the military hand.

   B. Who asked a question in verse 2, and what did he ask?

   _____

   _____

   C. What is the dilemma, and how did John respond (vv. 3–4)?

   _____

   _____

D. What did one of the elders tell John? How did the elder describe Jesus (v. 5)?

_____

_____

E. A parallel portrait of Jesus coming as a mighty military leader is in Revelation 19:11–16. Describe it. What characteristics does this portrait have in common with the Lion?

_____

_____

In Psalm 45 you also see the Bridegroom leading the military against the enemies of God. "Jesus," the Reformed Bible explains, "leads the church against demonic forces and will return again to destroy all evil."[11]

F. What are some enemies you are eager to see defeated in that great and terrible day?

_____

_____

G. What opposite portrait of *The Lion* appears in Revelation 5:6?

_____

_____

H. What do you think is the significance of the Lion and the Lamb being portrayed so closely together?

_____

_____

I. What else do you learn about the Lamb from Revelation 5:7–14?

_____

_____

J. What significance do you see in the Lamb's being both slain and alive?

_____

_____

Review

As you review this week and the portrait of Jesus as the Lion, what truths do you want to remember?

Take one of these truths and apply it to your life right now.

Prayer Time

As much as possible, break into the same groups as last week's and be accountable to one another.

In prayer, share praises for areas where you see your chains being broken. Or confess your sin and ask God to release you again. If you were not here last week, ask for help in an area where you are weak and have the others support you. (Look at last week's Prayer Time.)

Remember to keep "burying your face in His mane" and asking Him to fill you with Lion-strength. Make this a pattern of your life.

Close with the second verse to "A Mighty Fortress Is Our God." The title "Lord Sabaoth" has to do with being the military leader of all the good angels, of all the bad angels. He is the King!

> Did we in our own strength confide,
> Our striving would be losing;
> Were not the right Man on our side,
> The Man of God's own choosing,
> Dost ask who that may be?
> Christ Jesus, it is He—
> Lord Sabaoth, His name,
> From age to age the same,
> And He must win the battle.

The Way, the Truth, and the Life
Artist: Martin French (www.martinfrench.com)

Week 9
THE WAY, THE TRUTH, AND THE LIFE

Jesus claims to be the only way. This exclusiveness is contained in this dramatic statement: "No one comes to the Father, but by me." That's on a collision course with all of the pluralism that we hear in America.

—R. C. SPROUL

MEMORY VERSE:
JOHN 14:6

*O*ur first portrait in this workbook was *The Great I AM*. In closing, we return to *The Great I AM*, but we will particularly focus on the specific portrait that is so relevant to all we have studied: *I AM the Way, the Truth, and the Life*. It is the heart of Hosea, the heart of John, and the concept that, as R. C. Sproul says, is on a "crash collision with all of the pluralism that we hear in America."[1] But embracing it, and embracing it fully, makes the difference between life and death—not only in the future, but right here, right now. Do we truly understand that a deep and exclusive love relationship with Jesus is the *only* way to live fruitfully on a daily basis?

VIDEO NOTES FOR WEEK 9

Watch the video first, and then put your chairs in a circle to discuss this lesson.

1. "I AM the Way."

   Paul Little made the analogy to jumping out of an airplane with a <u>b</u>_____

   _____. You can believe with your whole heart, but you will still perish.

2. "I AM the Truth."

   The truth is our <u>f</u>_____.

3. "I AM the Life."

4. In John's gallery, Jesus said, "I am the true _____" (John 15:1).

5. Hosea's gallery closes with "I am like a green _____ tree" (Hosea 14:8 NIV).

WARM UP

Can you think of one way the truth of the Scripture has been your friend? Explain.

Day 1

In Christ Alone

Judaism and Christianity are exclusive. All of the other religions, according to Daniel Doriani, leading professor at Covenant Seminary in St. Louis, are syncretistic. Doriani explains that the word *syncretism* is derived from the words translated "sin" and "creed."[2] How clearly this is painted in Hosea, for the bride, instead of "forsaking all others," welcomed "other gods in her bed." The exclusivism of our faith sets Christianity apart; it is also what causes the world to criticize us severely.

Our final portrait of Jesus as *The Way, the Truth, and the Life* emphasizes that Christ, and Christ alone, is our salvation. This is the pervasive theme in Scripture. As you read through the Old Testament, you will see that the Israelites continually struggled with letting go of other gods. Even good kings had trouble tearing down the high places of idol worship for fear of the rebellion of the people. Hosea is the book that gives us such a clear picture of this, when God characterized Israel as an unfaithful bride. The irony is that the people were "religious," celebrating the holidays and making sacrifices to God, but they were not exclusive in their devotion. Likewise, many in John's gospel were religious, but they had missed the heart of God by settling for religious activity instead of loving Him with all their hearts, souls, and minds.

Today we will begin with a review of the problem, and then we will look, for the rest of the week, at the solution.

1. What message was the Lord giving through each of the following passages in Hosea?
   A. Hosea 1:2

   _____

   _____

   B. Hosea 2:2

   _____

   _____

C. Hosea 2:12–13

_____

_____

D. Hosea 2:16–17

_____

_____

E. Hosea 2:21–23

_____

_____

2. What message was the Lord giving through each of these passages in John?
   A. John 1:1–4

_____

_____

   B. John 2:13–17

_____

_____

   C. John 3:16–19

_____

_____

   D. John 10:7–10

_____

_____

   E. John 14:6

_____

_____

   F. John 15:5–8

_____

_____

_____

Day 2

The Watershed Issue

Sing "Above All" or another worship song.

As you memorize this week's key passage, pray through the verse.

R. C. Sproul remembers an experience when he was a freshman in college. His professor was berating Christians because of their belief that Jesus is the only way to God. Abruptly he turned the spotlight on Sproul and asked, "Sproul—do you think Jesus is the only way to God?"

Sproul squirmed. If he said no, he would be betraying God. If he said yes, everyone would see him as a bigot. Softly, Sproul said, "Yes."

The professor turned his fury on the young student. "Jesus the only way? How arrogant, how closed-minded, how ridiculous!" The rest of the hour the professor devoted to belittling Sproul. How terrible is this claim of Christ. And yet . . . how wonderful.

At the end of class, as the other students filed out, Sproul sat quietly, asking God for wisdom and composure. Finally he picked up his books and approached his professor respectfully.

"Sir, do you think Jesus could be one way to God?"

"Well, yes, Jesus could be one way."

"Sir, if you believe Jesus could be one way and therefore began to study His life and His words and found that He claimed to be the only way—what would you do with that?"

"You would have a dilemma—but it's just so arrogant to say that Jesus is the only way."

Softly, but with a heart of gratitude, Sproul responded, "I'm just so glad there is one way."

His professor lifted his eyebrows, confused. With emotion, Sproul continued, "When I think of the price God paid—giving up His only Son, allowing Him to be beaten, mocked, and crucified—all to pay for my sin, I'm overwhelmed. I can't imagine going to God and saying, 'That's not enough. I'd like more options.'"[3]

1. Put yourself in the place of Sproul's professor. Evaluate Sproul's response to him.

   _____

   _____

   _____

The reason Christians can proclaim that Jesus is the only way is because Jesus, and only Jesus, is God. And once again, we proclaim it because He proclaimed it. The early Christians were not called Christians but "followers of the Way." Sproul calls this the "watershed issue." Jesus, and Jesus alone, is the Way, the Truth, and the Life. Let's consider the context in which Jesus made this dramatic statement.

Read John 14:1–6.

2. What commands did Jesus give His disciples in verse 1?

   _____

   _____

   _____

3. According to verses 2–4, for what was He preparing them? How did He reassure them?

_____

_____

_____

The Message paraphrases Thomas's response like this:

> *Master, we have no idea where you're going. How do you expect us to know the road?*
> (John 14:5)

4. Thomas was thinking in an earthly way. How was he misinterpreting Jesus?

_____

_____

_____

> Jesus turns a seemingly "geographical route" question into a spiritual affirmation. . . . The road that Jesus travels is not about location, it is about providing access to God for individuals.[4]

5. People often misunderstood the spiritual message behind Jesus's words. Explain how it happened in the following passages:
   A. John 3:3–4

   _____

   _____

   B. John 4:10–11

   _____

   _____

   C. John 6:30–34

   _____

   _____

In all of these, they thought Jesus was talking about the physical when He was talking about the spiritual. Likewise, Thomas was asking Jesus for a road map, and Jesus said, in effect, "I AM the Way. Guys, you are there!"

But the disciples still didn't get it. Can't you just picture them nodding their heads, listening to Jesus, whispering to each other?

"Did you hear what I just heard?"

"Is He saying He's God?"

"No—He's not saying He's God."

"I know He's *taught* us a lot of truth, but He's saying He *is* the truth."

6. What statement did Jesus make in John 14:7, and how did Philip respond? How does Philip's response show a lack of comprehension?

_____

_____

_____

7. R. C. Sproul saw this as the closest Jesus came to losing His patience with His disciples. What did He tell them in verses 9–11?

_____

_____

_____

8. Explain why this is the heart of John's message.

_____

_____

_____

Day 3

I AM the Truth

Sing "Open the Eyes of My Heart" as a prayer.

Continue memorizing.

(*Kathy*) As you could imagine, I sing many of my songs over and over again. I always try to sing the words as if I'm singing them for the first time so they won't get stale to me. I also am conscious of looking in people's eyes so I can communicate the words powerfully and personally. Well, the other night I was pierced so deeply by my very own lyrics:

> We live in a time when people are blind.
> They're not lovers of truth.
> They'll only believe what they touch and see
> and then think I'm a fool.
> My God is love—He also is holy.
> And in Him I'll trust.

I have been absorbing the news like a sponge on CNN. I find myself listening to what the right and the left have to say, but all it makes me want to do is pay closer attention to the ups and downs in my relationship with Jesus. Oh, how I cling to Him. Without His life, without His absolute truths, there are no boundaries or understanding.

Recently I watched Larry King's show. His guest was Bill Maher, one of the most eloquent and articulate men I have seen in these forums. Larry asked him all sorts of things on all different subjects. It always amazes me that Bill doesn't have to take a breath—he's right there with an answer. And boy, does it all "make sense."

Topics came up: Separation of church and state. Gay marriages. Abortion. As I said before, I can watch these shows with so many severe opinions and get awfully frustrated and sometimes angry, but somehow this particular response from Bill, when Larry asked him how he felt about gay marriage, sent a shiver up my spine.

> Listen, Larry, it's a no-brainer! Talk about religion and how stupid it is—it would not be an issue except for the Bible, except for religion. That's what is so bad about religion. The Bible is the problem![5]

May Jesus have mercy on our souls.

If only people knew who they were really dealing with. They have no idea who they are pointing their fingers at. It's just like Jesus to wait for a time to reveal His justice, power, and righteousness. We saw it when He hung on the cross. As He hung dying, He could have struck everyone mocking Him dead in a millisecond. But He didn't—because of love.

Francis Schaeffer, a twentieth-century theologian, describes in his book *The God Who Is There* a shift in thinking about truth in our world. The belief that there is no definable truth is what Schaeffer calls "the line of despair." This is not a place where people wallow in sadness but a place where truth cannot be defined. Above the line of despair people can say with conviction, "This is right," or "That can't be true." But below the line, they can no longer recognize truth.

Schaeffer says that Europeans dropped below the line of despair after 1890, and Americans after 1930. Today, whatever you believe is true, and people consider you judgmental to tell someone that premarital sex, homosexuality, abortion, or a multitude of other choices is wrong.

People often quote this scripture out of context: "Judge not, that you be not judged" (Matthew 7:1). Let's consider the context.

1. Read Matthew 7:1–5.
   A. What statement did Jesus make in verse 1?

   _____

   _____

   B. What warning and illustration of the warning did He give in verses 2–4?

   _____

   _____

C. What should you consider when you are judging your brother's sin?

_____

_____

2. Read Matthew 7:13–23.
   A. What did Jesus say in verses 13–14?

   _____

   _____

   B. Many who claim to be Christians are not. Why did Jesus tell us that we need to judge, or discern, in these situations (v. 15)?

   _____

   _____

   C. How did Jesus tell us to discern what is false and what is true (vv. 16–20)?

   _____

   _____

   D. What warning did Jesus give in verses 21–23?

   _____

   _____

3. Read 1 Corinthians 5:9–13 and summarize whom we are to judge and whom we are not to judge, and why.

   _____

   _____

   _____

4. Read Matthew 13:24–30. What is the main point of this parable?

   _____

   _____

   _____

5. What instructions did Paul give in Ephesians 5:8–11? How must we employ judgment here?

   _____

   _____

   _____

6. How would you summarize Jesus's teaching about judging?

   _____

   _____

   _____

7. Why is it important to let people know that our basis for right and wrong is not our own opinion, but the words of Scripture?

_____

_____

_____

8. Respond to the following statement in love and in truth. "The Bible is an ancient book full of myths and mistakes."

_____

_____

_____

One good resource for these issues is *A Ready Defense* by Josh McDowell. The first section deals with the Bible's reliability. Another excellent resource, though more academic, is *Redemptive History and the New Testament Scripture* by Herman Ridderbos.

In addition to giving people facts, a personal testimony telling how the truths of the Bible have set you free is important. As Dallas Willard said, "Jesus is not just nice. He's brilliant." Willard also says that people think of Jesus in some sort of "feathery realm" that has little to do with them.[6] They see Jesus as an ethereal creature dealing with dogma and law, but not real, with life-bursting energy. Yet when you tell others how His truths have transformed your life in areas as relevant as anger, parenting, overeating, and depression, you may just get their attention.

9. What are some specific ways the truths of Scripture have been your friend and set you free?

_____

_____

_____

10. What does Hosea 4:6 say?

_____

_____

_____

11. What does John 8:31–32 say?

_____

_____

_____

(*Kathy*) As I grow with Jesus, I am learning slowly but surely that His truths and the Truth, Jesus, are my friends. I find myself having far fewer days where I'm butting heads with the things He has told me to do or the foundations of absolutes He has told me to build my life upon. I trust Him. In a time when people are doing "what's good for them," or what "makes them happy," I yearn to do what's good in His eyes and live in ways that make Him happy. This is so profound for me: *the Truth is our friend.*

Day 4

I AM the Life

Today and tomorrow, we'll talk about abiding. One of the best ways to do that is through worship. Sing to the Lord. Connect with Him before you begin.

(*Kathy*) My friend Valerie Clemente had her parents in town recently. Her mom is in her mid-eighties, and her dad is ninety-three. I love spending time with people of that generation, hearing their wisdom, their take on things, their stories from the past. Her mom used to be a dancer and is so elegant. Her face is delicately regal. Her dad is so feisty. You could tell he must have been a catch when he was younger. He made his living by playing guitar and bass in clubs all around the Northeast.

I knew he would be delighted to sing me some of the old tunes, so I asked Valerie to get her guitar out. Those old hands wrapped around that guitar, forming wonderful jazz chords, and he began to sing. I joined in, and soon Val's mom was singing along with a sweet wide vibrato. (Picture Katharine Hepburn singing.) They were back in time, and I was right there with them: "You Are My Sunshine," "Down by the Old Mill Stream."

The next day Val told me what a great time her parents had. She told me it was especially wonderful to see her dad come alive again. He'd been depressed, sleeping a lot. That very morning at Val's house he had told her mom he wanted to die. Her reply had been, "Paul, you can't die here. You have to wait until we go home."

We both laughed. As I thought about it more, I said, "You know what, Val? I think Jesus says that to us."

"What do you mean?"

"Well, so often we want to give up. We get tired. We accept that life is just too hard. We live in a slumberlike state—a deadness . . .

"I think the Lord says, '*You can't die here. You have to wait until you go home.*'

"And even then, when we go home, it is only a passing away of our mortal bodies. Death to life. But we can't die now. Jesus came that we would have life—and He meant here and now!"

We love the portrait *The Way, the Truth, and the Life* by Martin French. In John, Jesus said, "I am the . . . vine" (15:1). In Hosea He said, "I am like a green pine tree" (14:8 NIV). He is the source of life, and Jesus offers us this life every day. We have everything we need in Him to live an abundant life. Oh how we often miss the blessings of His riches!

1. Two other of the eight "I AMs" refer to the life that Jesus breathes into us, not only eternally, but right now, right here. The first is in John 11:17–27.

   A. When Jesus arrived at the home of Mary and Martha, how long had their brother, Lazarus, been in the tomb?

     _____

     _____

   B. Describe the dialogue between Jesus and Martha in verses 20–24. What did Jesus tell Martha, and what did she think He meant?

     _____

     _____

   C. What great "I AM" statement did Jesus make in verse 25?

     _____

     _____

   D. What do you think Jesus meant when He said, "And whoever lives and believes in me will never die" (v. 26 NIV)?

     _____

     _____

Since believers do experience physical death, this is likely a reference to spiritual life, which begins at salvation and continues on. If you know Jesus, this life is in you now! He is the Way, the Truth, and the Life.

The last of the great "I AM" sayings in John is also a statement of Jesus's being the only true source of life. He said, "[I AM] the true vine" (John 15:1). God had blessed Israel, and He often likened it to a fruitful vine or a vineyard in the Old Testament (Psalm 80; Isaiah 5; Jeremiah 2:21), but Israel was far from God. Hosea described God's people like this:

> Israel was once a lush vine,
>   bountiful in grapes.
> The more lavish the harvest,
>   the more promiscuous the worship. (Hosea 10:1 MSG)

The more God blessed, the more they sinned. Did they truly know Him? Some did, and some did not. As you will see in John 15, some "branches" (those who appear to know the Lord but do not really) will be thrown into the fire. Others, who bear some fruit, will be pruned, so they will bear more. The pruning, as in the case of the people in Hosea, may be severe.

2. How did Hosea describe Israel in Hosea 10:1? Where did they go wrong?

     _____

     _____

3. Think about some specific ways God has blessed you. How have you used those blessings?

_____

_____

_____

4. Read John 15:1–8.

A. According to verses 1–2, what actions does God take with fruitless and fruitful branches? Why?

_____

_____

B. What is the condition for fruit bearing according to verses 4–5?

_____

_____

C. What promise did Jesus give in verse 7? What do you think this means?

_____

_____

D. What is the purpose of fruit bearing according to verse 8?

_____

_____

Day 5

I Am Like a Green Pine Tree

Ask Him to "kiss you with the kisses of His mouth" and have a sense of expectation as you study.

In John, the Lord likened Himself to a vine and His Father to the vine dresser. In Hosea, the Lord likened Himself to a "green pine tree." This beautiful passage closes the book of Hosea.

> *O Ephraim, what more have I to do with idols?*
> *I will answer him and care for him.*
> *I am like a green pine tree;*
> *your fruitfulness comes from me.* (Hosea 14:8 NIV)

Look at the poignancy and hope in this passage. How clearly we see the Lord's heart for us. His cry, "O Ephraim!" is like David's cry, "O Absalom my son, my son!" (2 Samuel 18:33).

1. What evidence do you find of God's heart for His people in the following passages?
   A. Hosea 11:1–4

   _____

   _____

   B. Hosea 11:8

   _____

   _____

   C. Hosea 14:8

   _____

   _____

   D. Matthew 23:37

   _____

   _____

(Dee) Whenever the Lord uses the name Ephraim to refer to His people, warm memories and emotions flood my heart. My mind goes back to the little village where I spent summers as a child, and to which I still go every summer: Ephraim, Wisconsin. There I made Indian forts beneath its towering pine trees, swam in its blue waters, and picked cherries from its lush orchards. This resort town was settled by believers who chose a biblical name (like Goshen, Illinois; Bethlehem, Pennsylvania, and so on). As a little girl, I remember asking why this village was named Ephraim. These were the answers I heard:

> "It's in the Bible—and it was religious people who settled here. That's why there still aren't any bars in Ephraim."

> "I think it is in Hosea—something about green pine trees."

> "It means 'fruitful,' I think—and there are all these cherry orchards."

As a teenager, I remember seeing this verse monogrammed on our neighbor's martini glasses: "The drunkards of Ephraim" (Isaiah 28:1).

I was confused. Why was that lovely spot named Ephraim? As an adult I learned that the word in the Bible was a name both for God's people and indeed for fruitfulness. God longs for His people to be fruitful. I also learned that the little Wisconsin resort town was named by Moravians who were fleeing persecution, and when they saw that beautiful spot covered with cherry orchards and pine trees, they named it Ephraim and prayed their lives would be as fruitful as the land.

2. What significance do you see that Ephraim is both a name for God's people and a word meaning "fruitful"?

_____

_____

_____

The closing of Hosea is a summary reminding Ephraim of her heritage, her discipline, and her hope. God remembered how beloved Ephraim, or His people, were to Him:

> *I taught Ephraim to walk,*
> *Taking them by the arms.* (Hosea 11:3)

But even though God loved and had nurtured Ephraim, they were "bent on backsliding" (Hosea 11:7). When God realized He had to discipline His people strongly, His heart was torn:

> *How can I give you up, Ephraim?* (Hosea 11:8)

The anguish and tenderness in Hosea 11 is that of a father who dearly loves his child. He taught that child to walk, He saw her through the toddler years and cherished her. If only we would realize God always has our best interests at heart.

(Kathy) This fatherly picture reminds me of a hectic day when I was driving around town in an effort to accomplish endless things. I stopped for a traffic light, and a little girl and her dad walked across the street in front of my car. She wore bright red overalls, and her black silky hair flowed down her back. Her small, white sneakers kept pace with her father's strides. I smiled when I saw her tiny hand wrapped tightly around one of her father's fingers; I remembered doing the same with my father.

In that moment, I longed to be a child again. I drove on, thinking about my current frenzy to get things done: a woman on the go but still God's child. A sense of well-being came over me. And I wrapped my hand around God's finger. He sees what frazzles, frightens, and frustrates me. I took a deep breath as I remembered who I belonged to.

He is the Way, He is the Truth, and He is the Life.

3. In what ways is the discipline God's people experienced in the Old Testament an illustration of John 15:1–2?

_____

_____

_____

In Hosea, the prophet received hope for God's people through a vision of a day when they would finally come home, repentant, into their Father's embrace.

Ephraim shall say, "What have I to do anymore with idols?" (Hosea 14:8)

And in response, God said,

> *I will answer him and care for him.*
> *I am like a green pine tree;*
> > *your fruitfulness comes from me.* (Hosea 14:8 NIV)

4. How do you understand, on a daily basis, that your fruitfulness comes from the Lord? How do you flesh this out in your life?

_____

_____

_____

(Kathy) After twenty-five years of relationship with Jesus, I am still amazed when I experience the tender hovering of His Spirit over me. Music is one of the ways I experience this. Just like you, I have a handful of singers that do something deep in my soul. CeCe Winans is one of them. There's a famous quote from the movie *Chariots of Fire:* "When I run I feel His pleasure." I can honestly say that every time I've heard CeCe sing, I can sense God's delight in her. How well she is able to truly forget about all that's around her and simply worship the Lord.

At a recent event where both of us were ministering, CeCe took the stage. I was prepared to have a sweet time of basking in the presence of God. As she sang through the first verse of the second song, gratitude for all that God is came over me. I started to weep quietly, thanking the Lord for His love and provision for me. Before I knew it, I fell to my knees and then bowed my head to the floor, heaving uncontrollably. He was there. He was tender. And He was receiving my adoration.

As I continued in worship, CeCe began to sing "Alabaster Box," a song that tells about the sinful woman who was so thankful to Jesus that she poured her most precious possession, her valuable fragrance from an alabaster box, on His feet. I placed my palms on the floor in front of me, as if I were touching His feet. How great was His cost in rescuing me, but also in continuing to deliver me. The floor beneath me was soaked with my tears.

In moments like these, it's easy for people around me to suspect something is desperately wrong, but at that moment, everything was so right. He was hovering sweetly, wooing me once again with His love. He is the Way, the Truth, and the Life. I am so thankful.

Review

What differentiates Christianity from other religions?

Hosea looked forward to a day when God's people would realize the futility in trusting in idols and trust only in Him, their "green pine tree." How has this impacted you personally?

PRAYER TIME

Pray conversationally in small groups, reflecting on your answer to the last review question.

Aslan II
Artist: Sally Brestin (www.sallybrestin.com)

Week 10
REVIEW

Turn your eyes upon Jesus
Look full in His wonderful face
And the things of earth will grow strangely dim
In the light of His glory and grace.

—HELEN HOWARD LEMMEL

The most exciting part of putting together a puzzle is the very end, when everything is coming together. The pace quickens, the picture you've been longing to see emerges clearly, and the competitive camaraderie is fun! Review weeks are like that: exciting, fulfilling, and fun. You have an opportunity to help each other see the picture clearly, to have a few "aha" moments, and to have the truths engraved more deeply in your heart.

Often groups are tempted to skip the review, but that is like skipping the last twenty pieces of the puzzle. The picture will have holes.

There is no video this week, which will give you more time to share how God has worked in your lives. Ponder the previous video questions, go back and review the lessons, and then be as open as you can be. You may choose to divide this week into two weeks.

Day 1
Turn Your Eyes upon Jesus

Review your memory work from week 1:

> *Therefore, behold, I will allure her,*
> *Will bring her into the wilderness,*
> *And speak comfort to her.*
> *I will give her her vineyards from there,*
> *And the Valley of Achor as a door of hope;*
> *She shall sing there,*

As in the days of her youth,
As in the day when she came up
from the land of Egypt. (Hosea 2:14–15)

Sing to Him as in the days when you first were delivered from bondage!

According to John Piper, "Beholding is a way of becoming," and, "To see God is to be changed by Him."[1]

To behold Him
is to love Him.
To love Him
is to be transformed by Him.

1. Have you seen new truths about Jesus in this study? If so, name one.

_____

_____

_____

2. How has this truth impacted you?

_____

_____

_____

3. Explain why beholding Jesus can transform you.

_____

_____

_____

4. Look back to the portrait of Aslan, the lion from C. S. Lewis's Narnia series. In this portrait, how do you see both the terrible and tender sides of Jesus?

_____

_____

_____

_____

5. During this study, in what ways have you seen both the terrible and tender sides of Jesus in your own life?

_____

_____

_____

6. Review your memory work for this week. Describe the context of this verse in Hosea.

_____

_____

_____

7. How do these verses encourage you personally?

_____

_____

_____

8. What does it mean to you that you can find the same portraits of Jesus in both the Old and New Testaments?

_____

_____

_____

Day 2

The Great I AM and The Word

Review your memory work from weeks 2 and 3:

> Then the Jews said to Him, "You are not yet fifty years old, and have You seen Abraham?"
>
> Jesus said to them, "Most assuredly, I say to you, before Abraham was, I AM."
> Then they took up stones to throw at Him. (John 8:57–59)

> In the beginning was the Word, and the Word was with God, and the Word was God.
> (John 1:1)

Both portraits, *The Great I AM* and *The Word*, affirm the deity of Christ. *The Great I AM* hearkens all the way back to Exodus, when God revealed His name to Moses: "I AM WHO I AM." And *The Word* hearkens all the way back to Genesis when the Word spoke and there was light, there was life, and there were the first man and woman. Both *The Great I AM* and *The Word* are key portraits in the gospel of John because John's gospel is the one that shows us not so much what Jesus did but who He is.

1. What is the significance of Jesus calling Himself "I AM"? How did His enemies react and why?

   _____

   _____

   _____

2. List the eight great "I AMs" from John's gospel.

   _____

   _____

   _____

3. How does the "I AM" appear in the negative in Hosea 2? What was the Lord saying to His people?

   _____

   _____

   _____

4. Kathy said, "When my father and then my mother died of cancer, He showed me, *'I AM Father and Mother to you.'* . . . When I battled with depression and bulimia, He said, *'I AM your Deliverer.'* As I sometimes struggle with my singleness, He says, *'I AM your Bridegroom.'*" Name some ways He has been the Great I AM to you.

   _____

   _____

   _____

5. List three important characteristics of *The Word* and explain where each can be seen clearly in Scripture. (We've gotten you started.)
   A. *The Word* is "God with us" (His supportive presence, as seen in Exodus).

   B. _____

   _____

   C. _____

   _____

   _____

6. How can you see both the terrible and the tender sides of the Great I AM?

_____

_____

_____

7. How can you see both the terrible and the tender sides of the Word?

_____

_____

_____

8. Can you share a way that the Word has been like the spring rain, bearing fruit in your life during this study?

_____

_____

_____

Day 3

The Master Artist and The Brokenhearted Bridegroom

Review your memory work from weeks 4 and 5:

> *He was in the beginning with God. All things were made through Him, and without Him nothing was made that was made.* (John 1:2–3)

> *For she said, "I will go after my lovers, who give me my bread and my water."* (Hosea 2:5)

> *Your love is like the morning mist, like the early dew that disappears.* (Hosea 6:4 NIV)

> *They did not cry out to Me with their heart when they wailed upon their beds.* (Hosea 7:14)

The same Master Artist who created the world, fashioning it out of nothing, is at work re-creating you, causing you to be a beautiful bride. The Master Artist is both a painter and a potter. As a painter He speaks in word pictures, and in Hosea He painted a full-length mural. As a potter He forms us on His potter's wheel, refining us through heat, shaping us into a vessel of beauty. Again, He did this in the story of Hosea. Hosea's unfaithful bride represented God's people, Israel, and every man.

1. Give some examples of pictures the Word has painted for you in the Bible, and explain why these may penetrate your heart better than simple statements.

   _____

   _____

   _____

2. As you review the pictures from Hosea that you memorized during week 5, explain what each was communicating. Then consider if there is an application for you.
   A. Hosea 2:5

   _____

   _____

   B. Hosea 6:4

   _____

   _____

   C. Hosea 7:14

   _____

   _____

3. Describe the full-length mural that Hosea lived out before the eyes of the Israelites. Include the children.

   _____

   _____

   _____

4. What are some of the key truths that you discovered from the portrait of Jesus as the Potter?

   _____

   _____

   _____

5. Looking back over your life, name at least one specific way He has refined you over the fire.

   _____

   _____

   _____

6. Key to the clay being malleable is water. The water of the Word must continually flow in our lives. How will you keep this happening, now that this study is at a close?[2]

   _____

   _____

   _____

7. In the lesson "The Brokenhearted Bridegroom," we addressed some common questions about approaching Jesus as our Bridegroom. How would you answer the following?

A. Is the portrait of Jesus as our Bridegroom scriptural?

_____

_____

B. Is there a sexual connotation that is inappropriate?

_____

_____

C. Isn't the bride simply the corporate bride and not the individual?

_____

_____

8. In Hosea, why did the Lord take His bride into court?

_____

_____

_____

9. What other strategies did He use to try to keep her from temptation?

_____

_____

_____

10. What was the role of the "friend of the bridegroom" in John? How does this relate to us?

_____

_____

_____

Day 4

The Betrothing Bridegroom and The Redeemer

Review your memory work from weeks 6 and 7:

> *I will betroth you to Me forever;*
> *Yes, I will betroth you to Me*
> *In righteousness and justice,*
> *In lovingkindness and mercy;*
> *I will betroth you to Me in faithfulness,*
> *and you shall know the LORD.* (Hosea 2:19–20)

And I will have mercy on her who had not obtained mercy;
Then I will say to those who were not My people.
"You are My people!"
And they shall say, "You are my God!" (Hosea 2:23)

How comforting to know that even though we have betrayed our Lord, He was willing to pay a price to redeem us, and He is able to continue to redeem us by giving us the qualities we need to become His beautiful and faithful bride.

1. What change of strategy did you see in Hosea 2:14–15? What have you learned about this passage?

    _____

    _____

    _____

2. How does the individual story of the woman at the well in John 4 parallel the story of the corporate bride in Hosea?

    _____

    _____

    _____

3. How has the Lord allowed you to go into the wilderness, spoken tenderly to you, and brought you out singing? Share one personal illustration.

    _____

    _____

    _____

4. Meditate on your memory work from Hosea 2:19–20, and share your thoughts.

    _____

    _____

    _____

5. Explain how the closing verse in Hosea 2 is such an important passage and how it applies to you personally. How might you use it in worship services? In your daily life?

    _____

    _____

    _____

6. Describe how Hosea was a redeemer to his wife according to Hosea 3.

_____

_____

_____

7. From what shame and slavery is Christ redeeming you?

_____

_____

_____

8. *The Redeemer,* another picture from John's "gallery," is the Lamb of God. What do you learn from this portrait of Jesus?

_____

_____

_____

9. What did you learn from Romans 7:14–25; 8:13 about Christ's power to redeem us from our chains? What is His part? Our part? How have you applied this?

_____

_____

_____

Day 5

The Lion and the Way, the Truth, and the Life

Review your memory work from weeks 8 and 9.

> *Therefore, since we are receiving a kingdom which cannot be shaken, let us have grace, by which we may serve God acceptably with reverence and godly fear. For our God is a consuming fire.* (Hebrews 12:28–29)

> *Jesus said to him, "I am the way, the truth, and the life. No one comes to the Father except through me."* (John 14:6)

There are times when God has had to be the Lion in the lives of His people because they failed to understand that He, and He alone, is the Way, the Truth, and the Life. Though this is a terrifying portrait of the Lord, again, it is important to understand that He acts only for our good; He longs to keep us from the destruction of false gods and to purge the spirit of harlotry from our hearts. When we understand that He, and He alone, is the One who adores us, who can meet our needs, and who will be faithful to keep His promises, then we can have faith to live each day.

John Piper writes that not only is "God most glorified when we are most satisfied in him," but also that this faith in His ability to satisfy us is the key to "emancipate human hearts from the fleeting pleasures of sin."[3]

1. Review Hosea 4–5 and describe the spirit of the Lord's people. How did the Lord respond?

    _____

    _____

    _____

2. Review John 2:13–17 and describe the people's attitude that caused Jesus to be angry enough to make a whip. What does this have in common with the sin in Hosea?

    _____

    _____

    _____

3. In what areas may you be disregarding God's holiness or forgetting Him?

    _____

    _____

    _____

4. Sometimes when God disciplines us, whatever that may be (a loss of His joy, the natural causative consequences of sins, or something more severe), we try to solve our problem in a foolish way. What did His people do in Hosea 5:13?

    _____

    _____

    _____

5. When you are sad or anxious, do you ever run to "false gods" who will only chain you tighter?

    _____

    _____

    _____

6. Review some things about the false gods in your life that should cause you to set your heart like flint *not* to run to them.

    _____

    _____

    _____

7. Review some of the things you learned about God's character that should cause you to run only to Him.

A. Hosea 11:1–4

_____

_____

B. Hosea 11:8

_____

_____

C. Hosea 14:8

_____

_____

D. John 14:1–6

_____

_____

8. What is similar about the promises the Lord made in Hosea 14:8 and in John 15:5?

_____

_____

_____

9. Trying to abstain from "false lovers" is usually unsuccessful unless you know you have a true Lover who can give you life, peace, and joy. Believing this will empower you to be faithful to Him. What have you learned about the character of Christ from this study that increases your confidence in Him? Take your time with the question, choosing the portraits that have been most meaningful to you and explaining why.

_____

_____

_____

We have intently beheld the portraits of Jesus from John and Hosea with you. We've stared and studied, pondered and prayed, and come out in awe of a God who is terrible yet wonderful. We all know that this life will continue to offer disappointments and deep sorrow. But whatever state of heart we find ourselves in, we can believe in the One who has professed to be all we need. He is the One we can count on. He is the One we can cling to. He truly is the Great I AM.

He's so close. Stay near His heart. He will never leave you. As He holds you through this life, the pain will pass, the tears will no longer flow, and death will be no more. What a wonderful place to be: forever in love with Jesus.

—DEE AND KATHY

Appendix A
WORSHIP CHORUSES

ABOVE ALL

Above all powers, above all kings,
Above all nations and all created things;
Above all wisdom and all the ways of man,
You were here before the world began.

Above all kingdoms, above all thrones,
Above all wonders the world has ever known;
Above all wealth and treasures of the earth,
There's no way to measure what You're worth.

Crucified, laid behind a stone.
You lived to die, rejected and alone.
Like a rose trampled on the ground,
You took the fall, and thought of me
Above all.

"Above All," words by Paul Baloche and Lenny LeBlanc © 1999 Integrity's Hosanna! Music/Lensongs Publishing/ASCAP/Used by permission.

A MIGHTY FORTRESS IS OUR GOD

A mighty fortress is our God,
A bulwark never failing;
Our helper He amid the flood
Of mortal ills prevailing.
For still our ancient foe
Doth seek to work us woe;
His craft and pow'r are great,
And, armed with cruel hate,
On earth is not his equal.

Did we in our won strength confide,
Our striving would be losing;
Were not the right Man on our side,
The Man of God's own choosing.
Dost ask who that may be?
Christ Jesus, it is He;
Lord Sabaoth, His name,
From age to age the same,
And He must win the battle.

And tho this world, with devils filled,
Should threaten to undo us,
We will not fear, for God hath willed
His truth to triumph through us.
The prince of darkness grim—
We tremble not for him;
His rage we can endure,
For lo! his doom is sure,
One little word shall fell him.

That word above all earthly pow'rs,
No thanks to them, abideth;
The Spirit and the gifts are ours
Through Him who with us sideth.
Let goods and kindred go,
This mortal life also;
The body they may kill.
God's truth abideth still;
His kingdom is forever.

"A Mighty Fortress Is Our God," words by Martin Luther (1483–1546). Public domain.

CHANGE MY HEART, OH GOD

Change my heart, oh God,
Make it ever true;
Change my heart, oh God,
May I be like you.

You are the potter,
I am the clay.
Mold me and make me;
This is what I pray.

Change my heart, oh God,
Make it ever true;
Change my heart, oh God,
May I be like you.

"Change My Heart, Oh God," words by Eddie Espinosa © 1982 Mercy/Vineyard Publishing (admin. Music Services, Nashville, TN)/Used by permission.

DRAW ME CLOSE

Draw me close to You,
Never let me go.
I lay it all down again
To hear You say that I'm Your friend.

You are my desire,
No one else will do.
'Cause nothing else can take Your place,
To feel the warmth of Your embrace.
Help me find the way;
Bring me back to You.

You're all I want.
You're all I've ever needed.
You're all I want,
Help me know You are near.

Draw me close to You,
Never let me go.
I lay it all down again

To feel the warmth of Your embrace.
Help me find the way,
Bring me back to You.

"Draw Me Close," words by Kelly Carpenter © 1994 Mercy/Vineyard Publishing (admin. Music Services, Nashville, TN)/Used by permission.

GREAT IS THY FAITHFULNESS

Great is Thy faithfulness, O God my Father,
There is no shadow of turning with Thee;
Thou changest not, Thy compassions they
    fail not;
As Thou hast been Thou forever wilt be.

Great is Thy faithfulness!
Great is Thy faithfulness!
Morning by morning new mercies I see;
All I have needed Thy hand hath provided;
Great is Thy faithfulness, Lord, unto me!

Stanza 2
Summer and winter, and springtime and
    harvest,
Sun, moon, and stars in their courses above
Join with all nature in manifold witness
To Thy great faithfulness, mercy, and love.

Stanza 3
Pardon for sin and a peace that endureth,
Thine own dear presence to cheer and to guide;
Strength for today and bright hope for
    tomorrow,
Blessings all mine, with ten thousand beside!

"Great Is Thy Faithfulness," words by Thomas O. Chisholm © 1923 Hope Publishing Company. Used by permission.

HAVE THINE OWN WAY, LORD

Have Thine own way, Lord! Have Thine own
    way!
Thou art the potter, I am the clay;

Mold me and make me after Thy will,
While I am waiting, yielded and still.

Have Thine own way, Lord! Have Thine own way!
Search me and try me, Master, today!
Whiter than snow, Lord, wash me just now,
As in Thy presence humbly I bow.

Have Thine own way, Lord! Have Thine own way!
Hold o'er my being absolute sway!
Fill with Thy Spirit, 'till all shall see
Christ only, always, living in me.

"Have Thine Own Way, Lord," words by Adelaide A. Pollard ©
1907. Public domain.

HE TOUCHED ME

Shackled by a heavy burden,
'Neath a load of guilt and shame;
Then the hand of Jesus touched me,
And now I am no longer the same.

He touched me, O, he touched me,
And O, the joy that floods my soul;
Something happened, and now I know,
He touched me and made me whole.

Stanza 2
Since I met this blessed Savior,
Since He cleansed and made me whole;
I will never cease to praise Him,
I'll shout it while eternity rolls.

"He Touched Me," words and music by William J. Gaither. ©
1963 by William J. Gaither. All rights Reserved. Used by permission of Gaither Music Company.

O COME ALL YE FAITHFUL

O come all ye faithful, joyful and triumphant,
O come ye, O come ye to Bethlehem!
Come and behold Him, born the King of angels!

Refrain:
O come, let us adore Him, O come, let us adore
    Him,
O come, let us adore Him, Christ the Lord!

Stanza 2
True God of True God, Light from Light
    Eternal,
Lo, He shuns not the virgin's womb;
Son of the Father, begotten, not created.

Stanza 3
Sing, choirs of angels, sing in exultation,
O sing, all ye citizens of heaven above!
Glory to God, all glory in the highest!

Stanza 4
See how the shepherds, summoned to His cradle,
Leaving their flocks, draw nigh to gaze;
We too will thither bend our joyful footsteps.

Stanza 5
Child, for us sinners poor and in the manger,
We would embrace Thee with love and awe.
Who would not love Thee, loving us so dearly?

Stanza 6
Yea, Lord, we greet Thee, born this happy
    morning,
Jesus, to Thee be all glory given.
Word of the Father, now in flesh appearing!

"O Come All Ye Faithful," Latin hymn, ascribed to John Francis
Wade. Public domain.

O COME, O COME, EMMANUEL

O come, O come, Emmanuel,
And ransom captive Israel,
That mourns in lonely exile here
Until the Son of God appear.

O come, Thou Dayspring, come and cheer
Our spirits by Thine advent here;

Disperse the gloomy clouds of night,
And death's dark shadows put to flight.

O come, Thou Wisdom from on high,
And order all things, far and nigh;
To us the path of knowledge show,
And cause us in her ways to go.

O come, Desire of nations, bind
All peoples in one heart and mind;
Bid envy, strife and discord cease,
Fill the whole world with heaven's peace.

Rejoice! Rejoice! Emmanuel
Shall come to thee,
O Israel!

"O Come, O Come, Emmanuel," Latin hymn. Public domain.

OPEN THE EYES OF MY HEART

Open the eyes of my heart, Lord,
Open the eyes of my heart.
I want to see You,
I want to see You.
Open the eyes of my heart, Lord,
Open the eyes of my heart.
I want to see You,
I want to see You.

To see You high and lifted up,
Shining in the light of Your glory.
Pour out Your power and love,
As we sing holy, holy, holy.

Holy, holy, holy.
Holy, holy, holy.
Holy, holy, holy.
I want to see You.

Open the eyes of my heart, Lord
Open the eyes of my heart.
I want to see You,

I want to see You.

Holy, holy, holy.
Holy, holy, holy.
Holy, holy, holy.
I want to see You.

"Open the Eyes of My Heart," words by Paul Baloche © 1997
Integrity's Hosanna! Music/ASCAP/Used by permission.

STEP BY STEP

O God, You are my God, and I will ever praise
   You.
O God, You are my God, and I will ever praise
   You.
I will seek You in the morning,
And I will learn to walk in Your ways.
And step by step You'll lead me,
And I will follow You all of my days.

"Step by Step," words by Beaker © 1991 BMG Songs, Inc. and
Kid Brothers of St. Frank Pub. Used by permission.

THE SOLID ROCK

My hope is built on nothing less
Than Jesus' blood and righteousness;
I dare not trust the sweetest frame,
But wholly lean on Jesus' name.

Refrain:
On Christ, the solid Rock, I stand;
All other ground is sinking sand,
All other ground is sinking sand.

Stanza 2
When darkness veils His lovely face,
I rest on His unchanging grace;
In ev'ry high and stormy gale,
My anchor holds within the veil.

Stanza 3
His oath, His covenant, His blood,

Support me in the whelming flood;
When all around my soul gives way,
He then is all my hope and stay.

Stanza 4
When He shall come with trumpet sound,
Oh, may I then in Him be found;
Dressed in His righteousness alone,
Faultless to stand before the throne.

"The Solid Rock," by William B. Bradbury. Public domain.

THERE IS A REDEEMER

There is a Redeemer,
Jesus, God's own Son;
Precious Lamb of God, Messiah,
Holy One.

Refrain:
Thank You, oh, my Father,
For giving us Your Son,
And leaving Your Spirit
'Til the work on earth is done.

Stanza 2
Jesus, my Redeemer,
Name above all names;
Precious Lamb of God, Messiah,
O for sinners slain.

Stanza 3
When I stand in glory,
I will see His face,
There I'll serve my King forever,
In that holy place.

TURN YOUR EYES UPON JESUS

Turn your eyes upon Jesus,
Look full in His wonderful face,

And the things of earth will grow strangely dim
In the light of His glory and grace.

WHO AM I?

Over time You've healed so much in me,
And I am living proof that,
Although my darkest hour had come,
Your light could still shine through.
Though at time it's just enough to cast a shadow
    on the wall,
Well, I am grateful that You shine a light on me
    at all.

Who am I that You would love me so gently?
Who am I that You would recognize my name?
Lord, who am I that You would speak to me so
    softly?
Conversation with the love Most High, who am I?

Amazing grace, how sweet the sound that saved
    a wretch like me,
I once was lost, but now I'm found,
Was blind but now I see.
And the more I sing that sweet old song,
The more I understand that I do not comprehend
This love that's coming from Your hand.

Grace, grace,
God's grace,
Grace that will pardon
And cleanse within.

Grace, grace,
God's great grace.
Grace that is greater than all my sin.

Appendix B
MOVIE NIGHT

—ᴄʒ

Rent *Tender Mercies,* starring Robert Duvall and Tess Harper (rated PG—ninety minutes). You will find it in the drama section at your video store, or you can buy it used online at Amazon, Barnes and Noble, or eBay (see week 1 for Web sites).

Just as Hosea married a woman with a tarnished past and restored her, so does Rosa Lee marry Mac Sledge, a man with two ex-wives and a history of alcoholism. As you watch, look for parallels between the biblical story and the modern one.

Afterward, discuss:

1. Did you like the movie? Why or why not?

   _____
   _____
   _____

2. What "baggage" did Mac bring into the marriage to Rosa?

   _____
   _____
   _____

3. What "baggage" did you bring into your relationship with Christ?

   _____
   _____
   _____

4. Do you think Mac was a backslidden Christian? Why or why not?

_____

_____

_____

5. What are some ways Rosa persisted in loving Mac?

_____

_____

_____

6. Share a specific way Christ has kept loving you, despite your failings.

_____

_____

_____

7. Why do you think Mac left Rosa and screeched off in his truck that night? Describe his pain, the source, and the possible ways he considered handling it.

_____

_____

_____

8. What are some ways you handle pain?

_____

_____

_____

9. Look at Psalm 25, which Rosa prayed through when Mac was gone. What significance do you see in this?

_____

_____

_____

10. How did Mac's past behavior affect his daughter?

_____

_____

_____

11. How did Rosa's love restore Mac and make him a different man?

_____

_____

_____

12. What do you think is the message of the closing scene where Mac plays football with Sonny?

_____

_____

_____

13. Where did God give Mac second chances? Where has Jesus given you second chances?

_____

_____

_____

14. What have you learned from *Forever in Love with Jesus* to help you with those second chances?

_____

_____

_____

_____

_____

_____

_____

_____

_____

_____

_____

Appendix C
LEADER'S HELPS

——⌒∾

Our prayers are with you in this important role. These tips will help you as you lead your group:

- Facilitate rather than teach, drawing out group members and rephrasing questions or pointing them to biblical text (What do you find in Hosea 2:15?) rather than answering for them. People remember best what they discover for themselves.

- Begin and end on time so that women will trust the time frame. Begin the video on time, even if women are still coming. Don't discuss any video questions, but answer at least a few of the Warm Up questions, and all the questions listed under each day. Mark other questions you especially want to answer, but don't feel that every question must be answered in group discussion.

- If you have a monopolizer, here are some hints:
  - Pray
  - Find ways to meet her emotional needs outside of group. Often women who talk a lot are hurting.
  - Don't sit across from her, thus increasing eye contact, but next to her.
  - Ask, "Can we hear from someone who hasn't had a chance?"
  - You may need to take her aside and visit with her, speaking the truth in love. Explain that shyer members need silences to gather courage to speak up, so you need her help to limit her sharing, or to draw others out.

- The main reason women drop out of groups is because they don't feel valued, so finding ways to show them love is important. E-mails expressing appreciation, the movie night, calls when they miss, and affirmation are vital.

Helps for Individual Weeks. The questions we see as absolutely vital are listed below, so mark those in your book as well as others you would really like to discuss.

WEEK 1: TURN YOUR EYES UPON JESUS

Hopefully someone else will say it, but if no one does, this is your chance to say that women who diligently do their homework ahead of time give one another a wonderful gift. Thoughts that have been prepared are richer. It is also true that women who make themselves vulnerable about their genuine struggles help the rest of the group take off their "masks."

If your group has trouble getting through the lesson in the allotted discussion time, answer only the questions indicated below:

Day   1: 1–6

    2.   They forgot God.

    3.   Isaiah beheld, then confessed sin, then was touched, then said "Here am I!"

    4.   Beholding affects the thought life and the heart. As we think, so we are. The heart is the wellspring of life. Concentrating on Jesus interrupts our preoccupation with ourselves. We become like the ones we love and with whom we spend time.

    6.   Consider how many things really have to do with the worship of ourselves: money, beauty, entertainment, the opinion of others.

Day 2: 1, 3B

    3B. This is an interesting verse, for Jesus divided the Old Testament into three parts: the books of Moses (the first five books, the Torah); the Prophets (which included not only what we usually think of as the prophets but some books we now classify as historical books as well), and the Psalms (which is the first book of what we now classify as "the wisdom literature" such as Psalms, Proverbs, Ecclesiastes, Song of Solomon). Basically, Jesus showed them Himself throughout the Old Testament.

Day 3: 2A, 2F; 3–4

Day 4: 1–4

Day 5: 1A–1C; Review question

Week 2: The Great I Am

If your group has trouble getting through the lesson in the discussion time allotted, answer only the following questions in addition to the Warm Up question and others you mark as a leader:

Day 1: 2; 3A, 3B, 3C, 3E

    3B. By showing them Jesus was the Creator, He showed them He is the Great I AM who made Abraham!

    3C. I AM the Light of the world, I AM the Resurrection and the Life, I AM the Way, the Truth, and the Life. Some may see others that lead to life, such as I AM the Vine, I AM the Bread of Life, I AM the Door.

Day 2: 3D, 4C; 5

4C. Literally: "I AM, I AM." Symbolically, God can compare Himself only to Himself because He alone is God.

Day 3: 2–4; 5B, 6H, 6I

5B. They suspected Jesus would not have her stoned, so they thought they could catch Him disobeying the Law. Instead, He exposed their sin.

Day 4: 1

Day 5: 1; Review question—Allow women to share one answer from this two-part question.

Week 3: The Word

If your group has trouble getting through the lesson in the discussion time allotted, answer only the following questions, plus those you choose:

Day 1: 1A; 2A; 2B; 3A

2B—The Word is both a message, as seen in the Old Testament, and a man, as revealed in Jesus in the New Testament.

Day 2: 7 (all parts); 8; 9

Day 3: 1

2. Truth confesses Jesus has come in the flesh. He was not just a spirit. He was fully man, born of a virgin. And when He rose from the dead, He was not just a spirit but had flesh and bones.

4B. How amazing is the pride of man. God "laughs" that man could attempt to plot against Him.

Day 4: 1; 2; 4; 5; 7

Day 5: 1; 4; Review question

Week 4: The Master Artist

If your group has trouble getting through the lesson in the discussion time allotted, answer only the following questions in addition to the questions you choose:

Day 1: 2; 3; 4; 6

2. The Word spoke the world into being.

3. God the Father calls Jesus "Lord" and credits Him with creating heaven and earth.

Day 2: 1; 2; 4; 5; 6

2. Because of our natural depravity, we easily construct a defense. But a word picture can penetrate our hearts before our minds can come up with excuses.

Day 3: 1; 9

Day 4: 9–11

Day 5: 8–10

7. This is one of the most difficult and, for many, disturbing passages in Scripture. Often the wisest response for those troubled by it is to acknowledge that it is true, but full understanding may need to wait until they see the Lord face to face. You can refer them to the R. C. Sproul book mentioned in the notes if they want to do more research.

Week 5: The Brokenhearted Bridegroom

If your group has trouble getting through the lesson in the discussion time allotted, answer only the following questions:

All Warm Up and Introduction to Bridegroom questions.

Day 1: 1; 3; 8

Day 2: 1–4

2. Unfaithfulness may be actual, or faithfulness is a grudging duty and the heart isn't in it. Though the partner may not be sexually unfaithful, there is unfaithfulness through lack of devotion.

Day 3: 1; 9

Day 4: 5 (Just those who wish to share)

Day 5: Review question

Week 6: The Betrothing Bridegroom

If your group has trouble getting through the lesson in the allotted discussion time, answer only the following questions:

Day 1: All

Day 2: 1A; 3C–3D

Day 3: 4; 5; 6

Day 4: 2A–2E, 2K

Day 5: All; Review question

2B. This passage contains hard truths. All of us deserve the wrath of God, yet God, in His mercy, chose some as vessels of kindness. For more insight into this difficult but scriptural truth, we suggest reading R. C. Sproul's *Essential Truths of the Christian Faith.*

WEEK 7: THE REDEEMER

If your group has trouble getting through the lesson in the allotted discussion time, answer only the following questions in addition to the Introduction Question and those you mark:

Day 1: 1; 5

5B. Just as Job said, "I know [rather than think or hope]," John assures us we can know that if we have the Son, we have the life.

Day 2: 2; 4

2A. Jesus is a "man of standing," a man who can rescue us, who is also related to us. He is our Kinsman, because He became a man through the Incarnation.

2B. Notice the chivalry, the protection, and the provision.

4. Hosea 3 is short and cryptic, so you might have your group read it in a paraphrase. You also have to imagine what happened between the lines, for this account is just the bare facts, almost as if it was too painful for Hosea to go into detail.

Day 3: 1–4

Day 4: 2D, 2J

Day 5: All (if time permits); Review question

WEEK 8: THE LION

If your group has trouble getting through the lesson in the allotted discussion time, answer only the following questions, plus the Introduction questions:

Day 1: 3–5

Day 2: 5; 7; 8; 10; 11

Day 3: 1; 4; 5A, 5C, 5D

1. This may be a new thought to many, so if there is debate, have them look at John 19:11 again. The point is not to minimize any sin, but to open our eyes to what we have failed to see seriously enough. When we repent of not loving the Lord, somehow the other things fall into place. When we

repent of not loving our brother, again, we find we are not breaking the list of sins God abhors from Proverbs 6:16–19.

Day 4: 1; 3; 5

2D. "Unturned" is half-baked. When we are not fully devoted to the Lord, it is as though the heat went out on our oven when we were trying to bake the cake. The cake is useless.

Day 5: 1F—J

Week 9: The Way, the Truth, and the Life

If your group has trouble getting through the lesson in the discussion time allotted, answer only the following questions, plus the Warm Up:

Day 1: All

Day 2: Skip

Day 3: 7–8

Day 4: All

Day 5: All

Week 10: Review

Hopefully, you can divide this week, but if not, mark the questions you feel are most beneficial for your group.

NOTES

WEEK 1

1. John Piper, *The Pleasures of God* (Sisters, Ore.: Multnomah, 2000), 20.
2. Henry Scougal, *The Life of God in the Soul of Man* (Harrisonburg, Va.: Sprinkle, 1986), 108.
3. C. S. Lewis, *The Lion, the Witch, and the Wardrobe* (New York: HarperCollins, 2000), 99.
4. R. C. Sproul, *The Holiness of God* (Wheaton, Ill.: Tyndale, 1985), 43, 30, 53, emphasis added.
5. C. S. Lewis, *The Magician's Nephew* (New York: HarperCollins, 2000), 70.

WEEK 2

1. Darrell L. Bock, *Jesus According to Scripture* (Grand Rapids: Baker Academic, 2002), 413.
2. Ibid., 408. "Christology" may be defined as the theological study of the person, nature, and role of Christ.
3. Eusebius as quoted in ibid., 407.
4. Darrell Bock and Eugene Merrill, *The Bible Knowledge Key Word Study: The Gospels* (Colorado Springs: Cook, 2002), 262.
5. In about 250 BC, the Old Testament was translated into Greek as well as Hebrew, so it is possible to see that these are the same words. The Greek translation is called the Septuagint.
6. W. Hall Harris as quoted in Bock and Merrill, *Bible Knowledge,* 261.
7. John Durham, *The Word Biblical Commentary* (Waco, Tex: Word, 1987), 39.
8. R. C. Sproul, "Before Abraham was, I AM," *Knowing Christ,* Cassette 6 (Orlando: Ligonier Ministries, 1999).

WEEK 3

1. Bock and Merrill, *Bible Knowledge,* 261.
2. E. Stanley Jones, *The Word Became Flesh* (New York: Abingdon, 1963), 2.
3. Bock, *Jesus,* 411–12.
4. Bock and Merrill, *Bible Knowledge,* 263.
5. Daniel Wallace, *Greek Grammar Beyond the Basics: An Exegetical Syntax of the New Testament* (Grand Rapids: Zondervan, 1996), 267–69.
6. Anne Graham Lotz, *The Vision of His Glory* (Nashville: Word, 1997), 194.
7. Bock, *Jesus,* 411–12.
8. Ibid., 410.

WEEK 4

1. Charles Spurgeon, "The Spirit's Work in the New Creation," in *Spurgeon's Expository Encyclopedia,* vol. 9 (Grand Rapids: Baker), 117–22.
2. "Introduction to Hosea," *Compton's Interactive Bible* software (SoftKey Multimedia Inc., 1994, 1995, 1996).
3. James Montgomery Boice, *The Minor Prophets: I. Hosea-Jonah* (Grand Rapids: Baker, 1983), 17.
4. E. F. Bailey, "My Name is Hosea," message delivered at Moody Bible Institute's Founders' Week, 2000.
5. "Hosea," *Compton's Interactive Bible.*
6. R. C. Sproul, ed., *The Reformation Study Bible* (Nashville: Thomas Nelson, 1995), 531.
7. Derek Kidner, *The Message of Hosea* (Downers Grove, Ill.: InterVarsity Press, 1981), 20.
8. R. C. Sproul, *Hosea: Part I* (Orlando: Cassette ministry of Ligonier Ministries, 2002).
9. Charles Spurgeon, "The Lord's Own Salvation," *The Charles H. Spurgeon Collection,* version 2 (Rio, Wis.: Ages Software, 1998–2001).

10. Kidner, *Message,* 23.

11. Boice, *Minor Prophets,* 21.

12. Spurgeon, *Spurgeon Collection.*

13. For those who want to study the scriptural concept of election (as seen in Hosea and Romans 9), we recommend R. C. Sproul's *Essential Truths of the Christian Faith* (Wheaton, Ill.: Tyndale, 1998).

Week 5

1. Derek Kidner, *Message,* 33.

2. Max Lucado, *When Christ Comes* (Nashville: Word, 1999), 144.

3. Kidner, *Message,* 33.

4. Ibid.

5. Tremper Longman III, *How to Read the Psalms* (Downers Grove, Ill.: InterVarsity Press, 1988), 23.

6. Sproul, *Hosea: Part I.*

7. Kidner, *Message,* 27.

8. Ibid., 27.

9. Ibid., 26.

10. Masonic Edition of the Holy Bible, under the heading "Light" (Chicago: Consolidated Book Publishers, 1963), 283.

11. Bock and Merrill, *Bible Knowledge,* 283.

12. Adam Clarke, *Clarke's Commentary,* vol. 5 (Nashville: Abingdon), 535.

13. John Calvin, *Calvin's Commentaries,* vol. 20 (Grand Rapids: Baker, reprinted 1999), 340.

14. Philip Yancey, *The Jesus I Never Knew* (Grand Rapids: Zondervan, 1995), 167.

15. Bock, *Jesus,* 423.

16. Yancey, *Jesus I Never Knew,* 169.

17. Bock, *Jesus,* 424.

18. Ibid., 115.

19. Darrell L. Bock, *Baker Exegetical Commentary on The New Testament: Luke 1:1-9:5* (Grand Rapids: Baker, 1994), 512.

Week 6

1. Spurgeon, *Spurgeon's Expository Encyclopedia,* 401.

2. Spurgeon, *Spurgeon Collection.*

3. Sproul, *Hosea I.*

4. Bock, *Jesus,* 435.

5. Ibid., 437.

6. Some have translated *Abba* as "Daddy," but it is more accurately "Dearest Father," a term of endearment adult children used as well.

7. Bryan Chapell, *Holiness and Grace* (Wheaton, Ill.: Crossway, 2001), 59.

8. Spurgeon, "God's Work in Man," *Spurgeon Collection.*

9. Kidner, *Message,* 34.

10. Sproul, *Hosea I.*

Week 7

1. Mike Mason, *The Gospel According to Job* (Wheaton, Ill.: Crossway, 1994), 215.

2. Ibid., 215.

3. Ibid., 215–16.

4. Spurgeon, "Exposition on Job 19," *Spurgeon Collection.*

5. Mason, *Gospel According to Job,* 218.

6. Ibid., 215.

7. Ibid., 216.

8. Walter Wangerin, *The Book of God: The Bible as a Novel* (Grand Rapids: Zondervan, 1996), 320–22.

9. Kidner, *Message,* 31.

10. Ibid., 41.

11. Robert Chisholm, *Handbook on the Prophets* (Grand Rapids: Baker, 2002), 347.

12. Calvin, *Calvin's Commentaries,* 126—27.
13. Douglas Stuart, *Word Biblical Commentary,* vol. 31 (Waco, Tex: Word, 1987), 67.
14. James Montgomery Boice, *Minor Prophets,* 36.
15. Ibid.
16. Spurgeon, "Christ Our Passover," *Spurgeon Collection.*
17. Bock and Merrill, *Bible Knowledge,* 268–69.
18. Spurgeon, *Spurgeon Collection.*
19. C. S. Lewis, *Prince Caspian* (New York: HarperCollins, 1951), 150.
20. Calvin, *Calvin's Commentaries,* 226.

WEEK 8

1. C. S. Lewis, *The Lion, the Witch, and the Wardrobe* (New York: HarperCollins, 2000), 99.
2. Leon Morris, *The New International Commentary on the New Testament: The Gospel According to John* (Grand Rapids: Wm. B. Eerdmans, 1971), 194.
3. H. D. M. Spence, *The Pulpit Commentary,* vol. 17 (Peabody, Mass.: Hendrickson), 87.
4. Darrell Bock explains, "What John has early in his Gospel, all other Gospels place in the last week of Jesus' career. Many simply argue that there was only one cleansing, almost ruling on the matter before considering the option of two cleansings. The accounts' differences do merit consideration that two cleansings are intended." Bock, *Jesus,* 426.
5. John White, *The Golden Cow* (Downers Grove, Ill.: InterVarsity Press, 1979), 7.
6. Bock, *Jesus,* 428–29.
7. Homer Hailey, *The Minor Prophets* (Grand Rapids: Baker, 1972), 151.
8. Boice, *Minor Prophets,* 53.
9. Ibid., 57.
10. Kidner, *Message,* 106.
11. R. C. Sproul, ed., *The Reformed Bible* (Nashville: Thomas Nelson, 1995), 802.

WEEK 9

1. R. C. Sproul, "The Way, the Truth, and the Life," tape 4 from *Knowing Christ: The I AM Sayings of Jesus* (Orlando: Ligonier Ministries, 2002).
2. Bock, *Jesus,* 500.
3. Bill Maher, interview by Larry King, *Larry King Live,* CNN, December 17, 2003.
4. Dallas Willard, *The Divine Conspiracy* (San Francisco: HarperSanFrancisco, 1998), x.
5. Bill Maher, interview with Larry King, *Larry King Live.*
6. Dallas Willard, op cit..

WEEK 10

1. Piper, *Pleasures,* 20.
2. Dee and Kathy are praying about what is next for them. Their desire is to continue! In the meantime, you may want to consider a study by Dee. A great follow-up would be *A Woman's Journey Through Psalms,* which studies ten psalms. It includes a CD from Integrity Music that sets those same psalms to music. Her *A Woman's Journey* series studies books of particular interest to women, such as Ruth and 1 Peter.

    Dee also has written topical guides on friendship, hospitality, and other topics (see www.DeeBrestin.com). Bible study authors we particularly recommend are Cynthia Heald (www.Navpress.com) R. C. Sproul (www.Ligonier.org), and Beth Moore (www.Lifeway.com). It is good to have a variety of grounded authors and also to study whole books of the Bible as well as topical studies.
3. John Piper, *Future Grace* (Sisters, Ore.: Multnomah, 1995), 9.

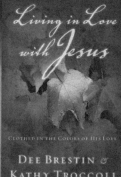

Week 1: Turn Your Eyes upon Jesus

Therefore, behold, I will allure her,
Will bring her into the wilderness,
And speak comfort to her.
I will give her her vineyards from there,
And the Valley of Achor as a door of hope;
She shall sing there,
As in the days of her youth,
As in the day when she came up
  from the land of Egypt.
(Hosea 2:14–15)

Week 2: The Great I AM

Then the Jews said to Him, "You are not yet fifty years old, and have You seen Abraham?"
Jesus said to them, "Most assuredly, I say to you, before Abraham was, I AM."
Then they took up stones to throw at Him.
(John 8:57–59a)

Week 3: The Word

In the beginning was the Word, and the Word was with God, and the Word was God.
(John 1:1)

Week 4: The Master Artist

He was in the beginning with God. All things were made through Him, and without Him nothing was made that was made.
(John 1:2–3)

Week 5: The Brokenhearted Bridegroom
(Learn all three word pictures)

For she said, "I will go after my lovers,
Who give me my bread and my water."
(Hosea 2:5b)

Your love is like the morning mist,
  like the early dew that disappears.
(Hosea 6:4b NIV)

They did not cry out to Me with their heart
When they wailed upon their beds.
(Hosea 7:14a)

Week 6: The Betrothing Bridegroom

I will betroth you to Me forever;
Yes, I will betroth you to Me
In righteousness and justice,
In lovingkindness and mercy;
I will betroth you to Me in faithfulness,
And you shall know the LORD.
(Hosea 2:19–20)

Week 7: The Redeemer

And I will have mercy on her who had not
*   obtained mercy;*
Then I will say to those who were not My
*   people,*
"You are My people!"
And they shall say, "You are my God!"
(Hosea 2:23)

Week 8: The Lion

Therefore, since we are receiving a kingdom
which cannot be shaken, let us have grace, by
which we may serve God acceptably with rever-
ence and godly fear. For our God is a consuming
fire.
(Hebrews 12:28–29)

Week 9: The Way, The Truth, and The Life

Jesus said to him, "I am the way, the truth, and the
life. No one comes to the Father except through
Me."
(John 14:6)